LEARN LIBRARY SKILLS SERIES

Learn ABOUT INFORMATION

INTERNATIONAL EIDITION

Helen Rowe

TotalRecall Publications, Inc..
1103 Middlecreek
Friendswood, Texas 77546
281-992-3131   281-482-5390 Fax
www.totalrecallpress.com

All rights reserved. Except as permitted under the United States Copyright Act of 1976, No part of this publication may be reproduced, stored in a retrieval system, or transmitted in any form or by any means electronic or mechanical or by photocopying, recording, or otherwise without prior permission of the publisher. Exclusive worldwide content publication / distribution by TotalRecall Publications, Inc.

Copyright © 2015 Helen Rowe

ISBN: 978-1-59095-433-1
UPC: 6-43977-44335-9

Printed in the United States of America with simultaneous printing in Australia, Canada, and United Kingdom.

INTERNATIONAL EDITION 2015
1 2 3 4 5 6 7 8 9 10

Library of Congress Control Number: 2015936637

Judgments as to the suitability of the information herein is the purchaser's responsibility. TotalRecall Publications, Inc. extends no warranties, makes no representations, and assumes no responsibility as to the accuracy or suitability of such information for application to the purchaser's intended purposes or for consequences of its use except as described herein.

The scanning, uploading and distribution of this book via the Internet or via any other means without the permission of the publisher is illegal and punishable by law. Please purchase only authorized electronic editions and do not participate in or encourage electronic piracy of copyrighted materials. Your support of the author's rights is appreciated.

TABLE OF CONTENTS

ACKNOWLEDGEMENTS ii
PREFACE iii
CHAPTER ONE Nature of Information 1
CHAPTER TWO Users of Information 9
CHAPTER THREE Information Literacy 15
CHAPTER FOUR Information Packages 29
CHAPTER FIVE Searching for Electronic Information 37
CHAPTER SIX Social Media and Information 53
CHAPTER SEVEN Bibliographic Elements 63
CHAPTER EIGHT Locating Information 77
CHAPTER NINE Presenting Information 93
CHAPTER TEN Libraries as Information Agencies 107
CHAPTER ELEVEN Different Library Environments 115
CHAPTER TWELVE Library Networks 135
CHAPTER THIRTEEN Other Information Agencies 141
CHAPTER FOURTEEN Client-Centered Information 151
CHAPTER FIFTEEN Information Standards and Ethics 159
ANSWERS 169
GLOSSARY 191
BIBLIOGRAPHY 200
INDEX 202

ACKNOWLEDGEMENTS

Thanks to Mary Gosling, Elizabeth Hopgood and Karen Lochhead who wrote the previous editions of *Learn about information*, and who kindly allowed their text to form the basis of this international edition.

Many thanks to my colleagues, family and friends who have offered their suggestions, knowledge and expertise in the updating of this publication. Thank you for your never-ending patience with me. I am also thankful to those students who have asked the questions to which this book provides the answers.

PREFACE

This book introduces basic information and skills needed by everyone who works in an information agency, such as a library.

The book is designed for use on your own or in a formal course of study.

Throughout the book you will find exercises to develop and test your skills and quizzes to test your understanding. There are answers for self-checking at the back of the book. Since some of the exercises relate to individual libraries and experiences, they do not all have answers, and some answers provide guidance only. You may not always agree completely with the answers given, and it will be useful to check them with an instructor or experienced librarian.

Note on Spelling and Capitalization

This edition is designed for use in North America, Europe and Australasia, across countries that employ different spelling conventions for English words. For consistency, American spelling has been adopted for the text.

Titles included in the text are capitalized according to standard library cataloging practice – that is, apart from names, only the first word of the title has a capital letter. This is intended to accustom library students and staff to this style.

CHAPTER ONE
Nature of Information

Introduction
The twenty-first century has transformed our culture into an information age where all we need is at our fingertips. Technology has changed the way we acquire knowledge and pass it on to others. We no longer need to accumulate all the information we may possibly require for a lifetime. Instead, we need to understand what information is, what it does, why it is useful, and where to find it.

This chapter broadly sets the scene by discussing the nature of information and its characteristics.

What is Information?
Information is data that has been analyzed and organized to be meaningful to the person receiving it. When it is accepted, information leads to knowledge.

Data is defined as recorded facts and figures (e.g., cost of raw materials, client statistics) that result from observation, surveys or research. Data describes rather than evaluates. Data is sometimes referred to as metadata or data about data.

Knowledge is data that an individual recognizes as relevant and is thought about, interpreted, stored (in one's memory or in a variety of formats) or used for a purpose. That is, it has been transformed into information.

Information is the result of analysis, synthesis and evaluation based on available data. In other words, the data has been:
- organized
- structured
- considered
- communicated.

Information can consist of a range of formats of material and can come in the form of data, images, text, documents and/or sound.

EXERCISE 1.1

Answer the following questions about information.

1. What do you think of when you hear or read the word 'information'?

2. Here are some dictionary definitions of 'information'. Do you agree with these?

    Knowledge communicated or received concerning some fact or circumstance; news.
    (*Macquarie dictionary*: http://www.macquariedictionary.com.au/)

    Facts provided or learned about something or someone
    (*Oxford dictionary*: http://www.oxforddictionaries.com)

    Knowledge obtained from investigation, study or instruction
    (*Merriam-Webster online dictionary*: http://www.merriam-webster.com/)

    Something told; news; intelligence; word; any data that can be stored in and retrieved from a computer
    (*Collins dictionary:* http://www.collinsdictionary.com)

3. Does the term 'information' now need a more complex definition? Why or why not?

Communication

Information gathering and transmitting are almost as old as civilization itself. Consider the development of human communications:
- cave paintings with symbols representing knowledge
- the development of writing which enabled humans to accumulate and pass on information (e.g., Egyptian hieroglyphics; Greek and Roman alphabets developed to transmit messages, texts and numbers; Eastern scripts)
- the invention of the printing press (1456) and the subsequent gradual spread of literacy
- the explosion of information that has led to the development of technologies to store and retrieve that information.

Today it is extremely important to be able to access and use information effectively and efficiently—that is, to be 'information literate'.

Characteristics of Information

Information is often described as a commodity. It can be bought and sold, exchanged, accumulated and stored, patented and owned—but it is not depleted when used. Often the use of information actually expands it. This is apparent in the growth and acceptance of the information source *Wikipedia* (http://www.wikipedia.org). The potential demand for information is unlimited.

Information is considered to be a personal, organizational and national resource of great value. The economy is based not only on industry and physical resources, but also on information.

Information is most valuable when it is quickly and easily available and effectively organized. Its importance to the user is relative and depends on changing situations, times and needs.

Why Seek Information?

We look for information:
- to gain knowledge
- to collect data
- to solve problems.

If we seek information, and get it, we can make better decisions. If we don't have any information, the chance of making a good decision is poor. If the information we obtain isn't good, the chance of making a good decision is once again poor. We need adequate and quality information to make a good decision, otherwise we risk making a bad one.

What is Good Information?

Relevant: Information must relate to an individual's needs. In theory all the information required to meet the user's purposes must be available.

Timely: Information must be available when it is needed, within the timeframe desired by the user.

Accurate and complete: All available information should be accessible, with emphasis on the 'right' information. This usually depends on the context.

Concise: Information must be understandable to those who use it, so they can absorb it quickly enough for action.

Unambiguous: Information should clarify and enhance the user's understanding. A statement that is made should not be open to more than one interpretation. Therefore, good information should reduce uncertainty and meet a user's requirements completely.

The informed decision is the best decision. For information to be useful for decision-making, it must be:
- the right information
- available at the right time
- available to the right person
- at the right cost
- in the right format to facilitate a decision.

What is Poor Information?

Irrelevant: Information is of little value when it is not relevant to the user's need. This may occur when information is too detailed, or too general, or if it relates to a topic that is outside the scope of the information need.

Currency: If information is out of date, it may be old and not useful or correct. Information that has been superseded is no longer useful.

Voluminous: Information is not helpful when there is too much of it to allow a sensible interpretation to be made in the time available. It is the quality of information that is important, not the quantity!

Unclear: Information is poor when it is not presented in a way that will facilitate a decision or application.

Incomplete: When all of the information is not given it may fail to provide a clear sense of the entire problem and become misleading.

EXERCISE 1.2

Watch the news on TV and choose an item of interest to you.
Listen to the same news item on the radio. Find an article in the next day's newspaper, in print or online on the same topic. Locate a social media comment on the topic.
Compare the coverage of the story.

1. Which source provided the most complete information?

2. Was the information good or bad based on the criteria given in this chapter?

3. Did the quality of the information vary with the different information providers (television, radio, online or print newspaper, social media), or was it all the same?

Sources of Information

Information is derived from a variety of sources. These can be described as:
- primary
- secondary
- tertiary.

Primary
The primary source is where the information is generated, so these are original documents that contain first-hand information (e.g., letters, scientific discovery, collated data, recording of an interview).

Secondary
Secondary sources comment on events, discoveries etc. They provide an interpretation of information gathered from primary sources (e.g., textbooks, encyclopedias, yearbooks, commentaries and articles in a journal).

Tertiary
Tertiary sources are used to track existing information. They present summaries, condensed versions or overviews of materials, usually with references back to the primary or secondary source (e.g., indexes and abstracts, catalogs, bibliographies).

Creation and Dissemination of Information

Information is created in many original forms, to satisfy the creator and to suit the user. Once created, the information is disseminated using a range of media and means of transmission, including oral and print and electronic formats.

Take, for example, the decision about a nation's Davis Cup tennis team. The following steps are taken in the creation and dissemination of this information:

1. The managers decide who will be in the team. This is done by discussion (i.e., orally).
2. The decision is written down, probably by the secretary of the committee (i.e., handwritten).
3. This may be typed up for easier reading and distribution (i.e., printed).
4. The announcement is made at a press conference (i.e., orally).
5. At the same time, a press release is distributed (i.e., printed or emailed).
6. The press release is sent to journalists, who write a report then email it to their offices (i.e., computer or text message).
7. The news is spread via all the media (i.e., radio, TV, newspapers, magazines, the Internet).
8. The information is placed on tennis websites (i.e., electronic).
9. Interested people tell their friends, family, co-workers (i.e., orally or using social media).

CHAPTER ONE   Nature of Information   7

10. A history of tennis includes the names of the players. This is probably written on a computer, printed off in draft, photocopied to show to other people, and finally printed and bound (i.e., electronic, printout, photocopies, a printed book).

11. A book on the history of tennis is bought by many libraries, and its bibliographic information is found in local library catalogs and large national and international databases.

12. When other books are written about tennis they will include bibliographies that refer to similar publications.

13. Periodical indexes are published and databases are added to, citing newspaper and journal articles about tennis.

EXERCISE 1.3

Read the above example of the creation and dissemination of information. Decide whether the information about the subject is a primary, secondary or tertiary source.

	Primary Source	Secondary Source	Tertiary Source
1			
2			
3			
4			
5			
6			
7			
8			
9			
10			
11			
12			
13			

The Value of Information

It is hard to place a value on information because its value depends on the context and its use by particular users on particular occasions. Data and information need context and meaning to be understood. Information providers need to guide users to relevant information. In some situations they need to analyze and repackage that information.

Information is only of value if users can locate it in a form that is useful to them (e.g., if the information is only accessible in an electronic format and the user wants printed information they must be able to print it for the information to be useful to them). Problems arise if the information presented is carelessly assembled, false, misleading or biased.

In addition, the agency that provides information, such as a library or information agency, must be seen to be of value if it is to continue to exist. All information providers are required to justify their role and the level of their funding. They are accountable for the level of service and answerable for their cost-effectiveness.

REVISION QUIZ 1.4

Use the following questions to revise your understanding of the nature of information. You do not need to write down the answers.

1. Apart from text, what other methods are used to present information?

2. What are the five characteristics of good information highlighted in this chapter?

3. What makes information useful for decision-making?

4. Name three sources of information. What distinguishes them from each other?

CHAPTER TWO
Users of Information

Introduction
Almost everyone at some time or another has made use of information, and so can be described as a user of information. One of the important skills for work, for study and for everyday life is being able to locate the information relevant to your needs quickly and efficiently.

Major Users of Information
There are many kinds of information users who have a broad range of requirements for information. They can be categorized into users in:
- business and industry
- research and development
- education
- recreation.

The methods they use to locate information will vary from one individual or group of users to the next but, regardless of that, their need for that information will be there.

Business and Industry
Businesses need information about their industry for comparison, to generate ideas, and to motivate them. They need to track competitors and follow trends in production and in markets. Gaining an edge in information is crucial, so it is vital to access it quickly and efficiently. Success hinges on the quality of the analysis and the effective use of accurate and up-to-date information. This has led many businesses to create departments of information management that oversee the movement of information through the organization. 'Information management' implies the harnessing of all information from all sources, including information technology, records management, research and libraries.

Materials frequently used by business include:

company reports	directories
standards	statistics
patents	government documents
newspapers	periodicals
websites	stock exchange reports
online databases	telephone directories

Once businesses receive information, they consider its impact on their sector and location. Some of the information they receive needs to be kept and stored; other aspects are repackaged, with relevant data being sent out to others.

Information developed by business includes:

- data management systems
- material consumption records
- personnel records
- surveys of clients, products etc.
- technical reports
- production tallies
- sales records
- equipment inventories
- charts
- business documents
  - company reports
  - section reports
  - marketing documents
  - memos
  - emails

Many large businesses have their own libraries and computer systems to store and provide relevant information, and to access databases relevant to their interests. Databases regularly used by businesses include, among others, Ebsco's *Business abstracts with full-text* (http://www.ebscohost.com/academic/business-abstracts-with-full-text) that indexes key international business periodicals; the collection of journals published by Thomson Reuters (http://sites.thomsonreuters.com.au/journals/); and the many Reuters publications such as *Reuters business news* (http://www.reuters.com/finance).

Often universities with business programs offer specialist services specific to business (known as business information centers) and employ library staff who have expertise in this area.

Business users frequently request:
- company profiles and reports
- online searches
- reference books
- periodical articles
- media reports—TV, radio, newspaper
- current news items
- RSS feeds
- government publications.

Research and Development

There are many library and information networks that service research and development, e.g., the OCLC library network spread around the world, the CSIRO library network spread across Australia. Federal and state government department libraries as well as university research libraries have extensive information resources to support research. For example, the Canada Institute for Scientific and Technical Information (CISTI) is a major provider of scientific information to libraries internationally.

Users in this sector require up-to-date information and rely on services such as online newspapers, electronic journals, RSS feeds and other current awareness services provided by special libraries.

Education

Information is used in different ways in the education sector depending on the educational level of those requiring the information.

Primary or Elementary Education
At this level there is an emphasis on:
- learning to read and encouraging interest in reading
- basic skills using information and reference sources
- help using online databases and the Internet
- resources for teachers for class preparation and presentation
- statistical information on students.

Secondary or High School Education
At this level the emphasis is on:
- maintaining interest in reading
- more advanced searching skills
- assistance with preparation of assignments
- encouraging more independent research
- help using online databases and the Internet
- resources for teachers for class preparation and presentation
- statistical information on students.

College and University Education
At the tertiary level:
- Information is used by lecturers, researchers and students (undergraduate and postgraduate).
- Users need access to primary sources, textbooks, journal literature, a comprehensive reference collection and the latest technology.
- Help is needed to use online databases and the Internet to locate material.
- The increased availability of electronic documents has changed the way libraries acquire material and its uses by staff and students.

Recreation

Information is not just used for fact gathering. It can also be collected to give ideas and details to people in their recreational activities.

The recreation sector includes a large range of commercial entertainment outlets, newspaper libraries and, for the general public, the resources of the public library system. There are many websites devoted to recreational and entertainment pursuits, including fan sites, biographical sites and web pages with extensive search engines.

Users are often interested in media reports, reviews, and biographical details about people involved in the entertainment industry. Popular culture, sport and hobby information are other areas of interest with an ever-growing array of resources available.

Film 'buffs' constitute a large segment of recreational users of information. Major institutions that provide information in this area include the British Film Institute in the United Kingdom (http://www.bfi.org.uk/), the National Film and Sound Archive in Australia (http://www.nfsa.gov.au/), the National Film Board of Canada (http://www.nfb.ca/explore-all-films/), the Library of Congress Public Moving Image Archives and Image Center in the United States of America (http://www.loc.gov/programs/national-film-preservation-board/resources/public-research-centers-and-archives/), and the Moving Image Archives (http://archive.org/details/movies/v2) for archival material from around the world.

ACTIVITY 2.1
Visit a library or information service that deals with business, research, education or recreational users.

1. What types of materials do they collect?

2. What services do they offer their users?

3. Do these services compare with the characteristics outlined in this chapter?

Information Policies

Efforts have been made, at various times, for governments to develop national information policies (e.g., in Australia through the Scientific and Technological Information Services Enquiry Committee, in the United States through the National Commission on Libraries and Information Science, in Canada with its 'Connecting Canadians' initiative, and the United Kingdom government's National Information Infrastructure). These groups recommended that their respective governments adopt a National Information Policy which would recognize the importance of effective information services and would encourage the development of a national information system.

Library associations around the world have also been involved in making submissions to governments on the need for national information policies, raising the following issues:
- the need for community access
- education in the awareness of the value of information
- mass communication
- freedom of information
- copyright
- research and development.

However, the impetus to develop such policies seems to have faded in favor of policies related to specific types of information, such as technology, telecommunications or the Internet. There are many reasons why efforts to develop national information policies have been unsuccessful. Conceptually, it is difficult to define information and to obtain the agreement of the various interested parties. Politically, it is difficult to decide which part of the government bureaucracy should be responsible for such a policy, when several departments see themselves as players in the information industry. Many elements of a national information policy would also have implications for state, provincial, and local governments, and require their cooperation.

Information Policies for Businesses

While it has been difficult to establish national information policies, it is more common for businesses, government departments and educational institutions to develop information policies to deal with information management beyond the library level. Information professionals are being called on to coordinate the integration of information objectives and business objectives.

Information policies in business can provide a strategy for the management of information, including methods of acquisition and storage, how information is used, how it flows through an organization and how it relates to the organization's objectives. Information policies determine the coordinated control of information, the use of appropriately trained information managers and cooperation between different information sectors.

14 LEARN ABOUT INFORMATION

ACTIVITY 2.2

Locate an information policy at either the national or state level, or for a business, government department or educational institution, or one that has been proposed by a library association.

1. When was this information policy prepared?

2. What were the major recommendations of the information policy?

3. Has the information policy been implemented?

CHAPTER THREE
Information Literacy

Introduction
Information is used for many purposes: for work, study and everyday life. In order to use information effectively, it is important to become information literate. Information-literate people know how to find, organize, evaluate and use information effectively to solve a particular problem or make a decision.

What is Information Literacy?
In 1989 the American Library Association defined four components of information literacy:

> "To be information literate, a person must be able to recognize when information is needed and have the ability to locate, evaluate and use effectively the needed information."
> http://www.ala.org/ala/mgrps/divs/acrl/publications/whitepapers/presidential.cfm

That is, information literacy is the set of skills needed to find, retrieve, analyze and use information. With information literacy skills it is possible to engage in effective decision-making, problem-solving and research.

Information literacy involves knowing:
- what information is available
- where it might be
- how it can be located and searched
- how it can be retrieved and stored
- how it can be processed and presented.

Information is the key to so many aspects of our lives and it takes on many forms. It might be found in news, announcements, gossip, opinion, or published in documents. An important part of using information well is knowing where to look for the required information.

Exercise 3.1

Where would you find answers to the following problems? Do not try to answer the questions. Identify the information source or sources you would consult. There may be more than one answer.

1. What is the meaning of the word shindy?

2. I need a recipe for spaghetti bolognaise.

3. What is the quickest route to drive from London to Liverpool?

4. My toilet is leaking. Where can I find the name of a plumber?

5. Who wrote the book *The shipping news*?

6. If I am fined for speeding, how much will I have to pay?

7. I need the address of Kwik-Kopy Printing Centre in Toronto.

8. How would I obtain legal advice about a dispute with my neighbour?

9. My child has swallowed snail bait. What should I do?

10. Which bank will give me the best interest rate on a long-term deposit?

11. Who was Louis Pasteur?

12. My child is writing a report on snakes. Where can I find some information?

Information Skills

In order to use information efficiently and effectively, you need to develop information skills such as being able to:
- find information in a variety of formats (e.g., print, online)
- find information from a variety of sources (e.g., people, library, media, business, government)
- find information within sources (e.g., using an index, map legend, software menu).

Other important skills are being able to:
- ask pertinent questions
- select, evaluate and, if necessary, discard information
- combine information from different sources
- present the most relevant information
- present information according to the audience
- gauge the success of the presentation.

EXERCISE 3.2

How do you obtain and use information? For the situations in the table below, list any other information you need.

Planning a Holiday	For Employment	Applying to Study
go to tourist bureau for brochures	read newspaper	read course details

The Information Process

Researchers into information literacy divide the effective use of information into six steps:
- defining
- locating
- selecting
- organizing
- presenting
- assessing.

These steps do not necessarily take place one after another. When you have selected some material, you may need to locate some more. When you are evaluating the material you have presented, you may wish to go back to select some other material, and so on.

Defining - What Do You Really Want to Find Out?

This first stage involves deciding what information you need and why you need to find it.

In order to achieve this, you need to clarify the meaning of the task and decide what you need to do to fulfil the task. You might need to consult dictionaries or an encyclopedia to define some of the terms or ask a friend or colleague to explain what is required.

When Confronted with a Problem, How Can You Work Out What You Need to Know?
Before you start working on a problem you must understand the nature of the question. The words used to describe the topic indicate different approaches to the topic. For example, when preparing a report you may be asked to:
- analyze a situation
- argue a point
- compare similarities and differences
- define, describe or discuss a topic or idea
- evaluate a process
- justify your position
- illustrate your ideas
- review or summarize it.

You will need different types of information depending on which approach is required.

Types of Questions
The amount of information required will vary according to the type of question asked. The main types of questions are:
- directional - where are ... ?
- quantitative - how much ... ?
- factual - who, what, when, where and which ... ?
- reasoning - how or why ... ?

It is important to spend time ensuring that you understand the nature of the information you require. There are numerous ways to determine how to define a search and how to solve problems.

What Type of Information is Required?
- Do you need brief facts, definitions, statistical or scientific data, dates or concise outlines? Then use materials in the reference section of a library or search the Internet.
- Do you need detailed background information, in-depth analysis of a subject or various opinions on a topic? Then use books or journal articles.
- Do you need the most up-to-date information on a topic? If so, use the Internet, journal articles, newspaper reports or television documentaries.
- Do you need opinions or specialist points of view? In that case, contact government departments or other agencies, or search specific websites.

Locating - Where Can You Find The Information You Need?
In order to complete this stage you need to identify possible sources of information based on your previous experience and your knowledge of information sources. You might need to consult an expert or ask library staff for assistance in locating relevant information. It is important to record the details of any sources used, for future reference. Noting the bibliographic reference to the items you used, bookmarking or tagging websites, gathering citations in a database or photocopying title pages is advantageous. In order to work methodically and to save time, it is worth developing a search strategy.

Developing a Search Strategy
A search strategy is a plan for using the most appropriate sources as efficiently as possible. When developing a strategy you should:

1. Clarify the Problem
    - fit the topic into a discipline (e.g., computer science, history)
    - make sure you are familiar with the topic (check the terminology)
    - what level of detail is needed?
    - how much information is required?
    - what will the information be used for?
    - is recent material needed, or historical information?
    - do you need a particular format (e.g., a DVD or a periodical article?)

2. Select the Materials
    - decide whether the information is likely to appear in reference sources
    - determine if the information is likely to be held by a library, information agency, archive or other source
    - find out if the information is available on the Internet
    - consider whether you need to contact an expert in the field
    - choose whether you need to search the catalog, or consult indexes or databases.

3. Prioritize the Information Sources
    - identify the sources in the order of their likelihood to contain the information.

4. Locate the Sources
    - are they in the reference section?
    - are they held by the library or information agency?
    - will you need to find another location, such as the Internet?

5. Search the Materials
    - search until you find an answer or determine that the answer is not in that source.

6. Evaluate and Repeat if Necessary
    - is further clarification of the problem necessary?
    - is more time available?

When using a search strategy you need to ensure that you have understood:
- the type of information needed
- the formats (books, serials, company reports, electronic, graphic, aural, etc.)
- the method of presentation
- the timeline
- the resource implications
- any special sensitivities relating to the type of information needed.

Further information on the specifics of locating information is provided in Chapter 8 of this workbook.

EXERCISE 3.3

Choose one of the following topics, and complete the following using the resources in a library. Describe your search strategy.

Illegal immigration   Bill Gates
Memorial Day   Global warming
The Great Barrier Reef   Mountain lions
Scuba diving   Interior design
Italian cooking   Web page design

1. Find background information on your topic using a library's reference collection. Name the sources you used.

2. Locate two books on your topic using the library catalog. Write down the bibliographic details and the call number for each book and check whether the items are on the shelf.

3. Find the bibliographic details for two periodical articles on your topic using one of the electronic databases available in your library.

4. Use a search engine (e.g., Google) to locate Internet-based information on your topic.

5. Find the bibliographic details for two books on your topic using a publisher's website.

Selecting - What Information Do You Really Need To Use?
Once you have located some information, you need to select the sources and the information that will be most useful to you. You need to decide how up-to-date, how relevant and how reliable the information is.

Selecting an Information Source
All source material needs to be evaluated before it can be used. Some evaluation is done quickly because you can identify irrelevant titles or out-of-date publication dates. Usually you will have to skim through a source to judge its relevance, currency, credibility and objectivity.

Criteria for Evaluating Printed Sources

Author	The reputation of the author is a measure of a book's worth. You can check an author's professional qualifications in a biographical directory – e.g., *Who's who*.
Publisher	Check that the publisher is reputable.
Title	The full title of a book or an article usually indicates its content and purpose.
Publication Date	This will indicate how current the resource is.
Preface	This often includes a valuable overview of the content and purpose of the book.
Table of Contents	Chapter titles indicate the major topics treated in the book.
Abstract	Many journals preface each article with a brief summary of its content.
Illustrations	You can quickly flick through a book to see whether it includes pictures, maps, diagrams, etc.
Documentation	An author's notes and bibliography are an indication of reliability.
Index	The index will give you an indication of how useful a book will be.
Reviews	Reviews written by experts will give opinions about the book. Reviewers often disagree on a book, so it is interesting to find opposing views. Examples of book review indexes are *Book review index online* (which allows subscribers to link to full-text reviews) and *Book review digest*.
Expert Opinion	For some subjects it might be necessary to consult a subject specialist to obtain his or her opinion on a source.
Bibliographies	A selective bibliography on a subject will list the 'best' books on that topic.

How To Read Selectively
1. Look at the contents page; take note of the sections, headings and subheadings etc.; get a feel for the emphasis the book gives.
2. Browse through the introduction that gives an overview of the topic.
3. Look at the index using keywords relevant to your subject or topic.
4. Look at the bibliography to see what other sources have been used.
5. Skim through the book looking at its presentation and graphic material.

This will help you decide whether the book will help or not, or should be examined more closely.

Criteria for Evaluating Websites
Web information is not necessarily all 'good' information. Anyone can publish a web page; there are no required standards or rules to be met. So web page reliability and quality vary. It is very important to be able to evaluate the resources you find on the Internet—for yourself, and to assist your library's clients.

Many of the good sites are 'informational': sites whose purpose is to present factual information. Educational institutions or government agencies produce these types of sites.

Their URLs usually include .edu or .gov. Examples include pages detailing services provided by a government body or educational institution, and pages containing factual information such as reports, presentations of research, or information about a topic.

Criteria to consider in determining the quality of information found on a web page are:

1. Authority
   - Can the author of the page be determined?
   - Is contact information provided (name, email, phone number or address)?
   - Is the author affiliated with an organization? Or is the author speaking for himself or herself?
   - Are qualifications or credentials for the individual or organization provided?

2. Objectivity
   - Objectivity is related to authority.
   - Does the author have a bias or agenda? Is this bias stated or hidden?
   - Does the author indicate his or her goal in providing the information?
   - Is there a disclaimer included in the pages?

3. Accuracy/Coverage
   - Remember that almost anyone can publish on the Web.
   - Is the source of information provided?
   - Who is the intended audience?
   - What is the focus of the information?
   - What is the depth of coverage of the information?

4. Currency
   - Are dates (First Posted, Last Updated) included?
   - Is the information current or out-of-date?

5. Other considerations
   - Does the presentation appear professional (no typos, misspelling)?
   - Is the page easy to use and well organized?
   - Do the links from the page connect properly?
   - Is special software necessary to view the page?

Criteria for Evaluating Social Media Information

Social media allows us to share news faster than traditional news outlets. This means that social media can be a great source of information, even though the accuracy of the information shared through these channels is not always clear. With this, however, comes the need to verify and determine the accuracy of the information received, as rumors and misinformation can also spread quickly through social media channels.

It is therefore important to learn more about how people evaluate the information they read on social media websites. It is necessary to determine how they make decisions on the credibility of information they receive before they repost it.

When determining the authenticity of information found on social media consider the following:

1. Location of the source
   - Are they in the place they are tweeting or posting about?

2. Network
   - Who is in their network and who follows them?
   - Do I know this account?

3. Content
   - Can the information be corroborated from other sources?

4. Contextual updates
   - Do they usually post or tweet on this topic?
   - If so, what did past or updated posts say?
   - Do they fill in more details?

5. Age
   - What is the age of the account in question? Be wary of recently created accounts as they are likely to be opportunistic.

6. Reliability
   - Is the source of information reliable?

 Summarizing the process of evaluating sources:

- Information resources should be considered as 'evidence'.
- Viewing information as a tool to prove a point or support an argument is a useful starting point for evaluation.
- Don't assume that one format of information is better than others.
- All kinds of information should be evaluated carefully, including books, articles and websites.
- Evaluation is an art, not a science.
- There is no 'one size fits all' set of guidelines for this important activity.

EXERCISE 3.4

You have been asked to prepare a report on the use of solar power and need to find relevant information. After consulting catalogs and indexes you locate the items listed below.

Decide which items are likely to be useful and rank them in order (starting with the most useful). Give reasons for your choice. If possible, discuss this with your fellow students or colleagues.

1. An article titled 'System identification and model-predictive control of office buildings with integrated photovoltaic-thermal collectors, radiant floor heating and active thermal storage' from *Solar Energy,* volume 113, March 2015, Pages 139–157.

2. A monograph titled *Fundamentals of solar heating*, written by Richard Schubert and L.D. Ryan, that was published by Prentice-Hall in 1981.

3. An editorial from *The guardian* of July 7 2014 titled 'Solar has won. Even if coal were free to burn, power stations couldn't compete', http://www.theguardian.com/commentisfree/2014/jul/07/solar-has-won-even-if-coal-were-free-to-burn-power-stations-couldnt-compete.

4. Wikipedia article titled *Solar power* http://en.wikipedia.org/wiki/Solar_power, last modified on December 12 2014.

5. A pamphlet called *Get your power from the sun* published by the US Department of Energy, Office of Energy Efficiency and Renewable Energy in 2003 http://www.nrel.gov/docs/fy04osti/35297.pdf.

6. An article 'Potential for concentrating solar power to provide baseload and dispatchable power' published in *Nature climate change*, volume 4, June 2014, pages 689–692.

7. A Web article written for children, posted in 2010, titled *'How do solar panels work'*, http://www.highlightskids.com/science-questions/how-do-solar-panels-work .

8. A monograph written by Sandra Bright titled *Examining solar energy,* published in 2013.

Organizing - How Can You Best Use This Information?
In order to use information effectively, the final step in the process is to organize the information. You will need to arrange it in a logical sequence and may need to combine information from different sources.

Remember to record all the relevant bibliographic details of your information as you find it, not only to be able to check your information, but also to make it easier to compile a bibliography.

You will need to refer back to your original task to ensure that the information is relevant and to make sure you have covered all aspects of the topic.

Presenting - How Can You Present This Information?
Once the information has been gathered, it is time to consider what you will do with the information. Who will the information be shared with and in what format? As there are many aspects to be considered in this step of the information process, it is dealt with in Chapter 9 of this workbook.

Assessing - What Did You Learn From This?
At the conclusion of the information-gathering task it is important to assess whether you achieved your intended purpose. This includes reflecting on what you did and did not accomplish. It may be useful to ask questions such as:
- Did I fulfil my intention?
- How did I go—with each step of the information process?
- How did I go—presenting the information?
- Where do I go from here?

It may involve an assessment of:
- the information resources that you selected and their relevance to the topic
- your own strengths and weaknesses in specific information gathering skills
- how your knowledge could be improved in this area
- personal goals that may need to improve your information skills.

This type of self-analysis will assist you in strengthening your information skills for the future. You can reflect not only on what you have learned, but also on how you learned. This allows you to consider what experiences will be useful next time you are gathering information.

Information Overload
Information overload is defined as an exposure to, or the provision of, too much information or data.

A person can suffer from 'information overload', when they:
- do not understand the available information
- feel overwhelmed by the amount of information to be understood.

Some Reasons for Information Overload
- More information has been produced during the last 30 years than in the previous 5,000 years.
- More than 1,000 books are published around the world every day.
- According to the Guiness World Records, the Sunday *New York Times* on 14 September 1987 had 1,612 pages and contained 12 million words.
- The relative ease of producing and transmitting information.
- Social media has resulted in the production of an avalanche of emails, instant messages, tweets, Facebook messages and so on. This means that it is difficult to keep on top of the amount of information that is available.

As there is so much information available, it becomes increasingly difficult to find the particular information required. It is necessary to decide which information is useful, which is not, and where to look next if necessary.

Learning how to use and present information without causing information overload is a useful skill. Many people rely on information specialists or brokers, such as librarians and research assistants, to find, select and analyze material for them. Information brokers must be fully trained so that the information they present is relevant to the user.

Using the information literacy skills presented in this chapter will assist you to overcome issues of information overload.

CHAPTER FOUR
Information Packages

Introduction
It is possible for information to come from almost anywhere and be packaged in many different ways—in print, non-print and electronic forms. Traditionally, information was packaged in books, journal articles, and newspaper articles. Today websites, blogs, podcasts, videos and other forms of electronic media are also suitable places to find packages of information. Simply defined, information packages contain data found in resources that are in electronic, print, and non-print formats.

Types of Information Packages
The type of information package needed will change depending on the question being answered at a given time and the specific needs of the user. For example, when completing the crossword or sudoku over breakfast, or reading the sport pages on the bus, some people may find it more convenient to view this information on a tablet or laptop, while for others only the print version would be useful.

Electronic Resources
With the increase in resources obtainable via the Internet, much more information is available in an electronic form. Electronic resources are resources that need a computer or electronic device to access, manipulate, or reproduce them. Electronic resources are available in many different file formats and sizes. They are often presented as part of a web page (a document that can be read by a browser) or a website (a collection of related web pages designed to be used together). Examples include, but are not limited to: websites, online databases, e-journals, e-books, electronic integrating resources, and may be audio, visual, and/or text files.

Print Resources
Print resources are publications produced on paper and circulated in the form of physical editions of books, magazines, journals and newsletters. Print resources are packaged in different ways, depending on their anticipated length of life or permanency.

News, and other information which appears regularly and goes out of date rapidly, needs to be presented quickly in an inexpensive format. A newspaper or magazine is printed on low quality paper, is not bound, is intended to be read and thrown away, and is published frequently—daily, weekly, monthly etc.

Regularly published resources, called journals, periodicals or serials, contain information which must be available quickly but is intended to be kept as a continuing record—e.g., scientific or other research. These publications are printed on better quality paper, are often bound, and appear regularly—e.g., monthly or quarterly. In order to provide easy access to their contents, serials commonly publish indexes at regular intervals.

Books are usually published as a complete resource. They are also called monographs: mono (Latin) = one; graph (Greek) = write. Some monographs may be published under a collective title and these are known as monographs in series.

Non-Print Resources
Information packages may include many non-book or non-print formats—materials that require equipment in order to view them. Examples of non-print resources include DVDs, videos, films, slides, CD-ROMs, audiotapes and so on.

The table below provides several examples of information packages in electronic, print and non-print forms and their specific purposes. There are many more types of information packages, as you will see in Exercise 4.1.

Source	Electronic	Print	Non-Print	Purpose
Books	✓	✓		Extensive coverage of one topic or theme
Journals	✓	✓		Articles that report research
Magazines	✓	✓		Articles that report news or trends
Newspapers	✓	✓		Current events and news
Websites	✓			General information, government, personal or corporate data
Blogs	✓			Commentary on a particular subject
DVDs			✓	Storage for reports and information – text and visual
Maps			✓	Location of a place and navigational aid

Storing Information Packages

Libraries may house different information packages in different sections (e.g., a separate area for DVDs or maps). Users are often interested in a particular format. For example, a lecturer wants to demonstrate the technique used to take aerial photographs and requests a DVD on this topic, as another package would not suit his/her needs. Other users are more interested in the information and do not care too much whether it is found in a book, a DVD or a CD-ROM, as long as they have the hardware (equipment) to get the information from the information package.

EXERCISE 4.1

Decide which of the information packages listed below are print, which are non-print, and which ones are electronic. Circle the non-print examples. Underline the electronic examples. Look up the definitions of any terms you do not know.

archival materials
blogs
books/monographs
brochures
business records
catalogs
CD-ROMs
conference proceedings
DVDs
e-journals
electronic databases
ephemera
files/transactions
films
government publications
gramophone records
grey literature
indexes
kits
letters
maps

microforms
models
newspapers
oral history recordings
pamphlets
patents
personal documents
photographs
pictures
posters
radio programs
RSS feeds
serials/journals/periodicals/magazines
slides
streaming video
technical drawings
theses
TV programs
USBs
videocassettes
websites

EXERCISE 4.2

List examples of information packages that you have used in libraries and other information agencies.

Parts of Information Packages

Information specialists need to be able to identify the different parts of information packages, including the physical sections and the bibliographic details. For example, the author and title of a book are usually identified from the title page; publication information may be found on either the title page or the verso. It is common, however, for information to be provided differently in different formats of resources. Learning what bibliographic details are provided in different information packages and where to find them is important for correct citations.

Therefore, people who work in libraries and information agencies need to be familiar with the technical terminology and bibliographic elements that form the basis of all identification and description of materials held in their collections. Chapter 7 of this workbook covers bibliographic elements in more detail.

EXERCISE 4.3

The following terms are found in information packages. Using dictionaries, glossaries and your own knowledge, write definitions for each of the terms, and indicate what type of information package could contain each.

Appendix

Banner

Bi-annual

Bibliography

Biennial

Caption

Cartographic

CIP

Contents page

Copyright

Dedication

Dimensions

Discography

DOI

Duration

Dust jacket

Edition

Frequency

Glossary

Half-title

Hardware

Holdings

Illustrations

Impression

Imprint

Index

Introduction

ISBN

ISSN

Preface

Quarterly

Reprint

Software

Spine

Title page

Verso

EXERCISE 4.4

Choose three information packages, one electronic, one print and one non-print, and for each describe the type of information package, its characteristics, uses, users, whether it is easy to use and which types of information agencies are likely to collect it. (Refer back to the examples of information packages in Exercise 2.1 for suggestions.)

	Electronic	Print	Non-Print
Type of Information Package			
Characteristics			
Uses			
Users			
Ease of Use			
Types of Information Agencies			

CHAPTER FIVE
Searching for Electronic Information

Introduction
Increasingly, information is being created and made available electronically. A large proportion of this information is found via the Internet. The Internet is an everyday reality for most people. It has changed the way people find information, conduct their business and enjoy their leisure.

To take advantage of all the electronic information now available, it is important to know how to search electronic resources efficiently and effectively. This chapter covers ways of searching Internet websites and databases, and library catalogs and databases, to get the most from electronic information.

Searching the Internet
When searching for information on the Internet, if you don't know the address of the website you wish to look at, you will need to use a search engine or an online portal to find the address.

Internet Search Engines
An Internet search engine is a software program that searches documents on the Internet for specified keywords. It returns a list of the documents, known as 'hits', where the keywords were found. A search engine does not search directly across all the documents on the Internet, instead it searches a database of web pages that it has harvested and cached. Clicking on a link in the search results retrieves the current version of the page.

Search engine databases are compiled by computer robot programs called spiders. They 'crawl' the Internet, and find potential pages by following the links in the pages they already have in their database. Therefore, if a web page is not linked to another page, search engine spiders cannot find it.

Once a spider finds a page, it is passed to another computer program for 'indexing'. This program identifies the text, links, and other content in the page and stores it in the search engine's database. The database can then be searched by keyword or advanced search options, and the page will be found if the search matches its content.

However, there are some databases on the Internet, including library catalogs and journal databases, that cannot be accessed through general search engines. These types of sites are referred to as the 'invisible web' or the 'deep web'. The invisible web includes websites and databases with restricted access that need a login and password (e.g., intranets, subscription databases, member only sites). To search these databases, you need to browse the website that provides a portal to the database. The advantage to this approach is that you can use search tools that were specifically designed for that database to query information in it. The disadvantage is that you need to locate the database in the first place and the search engines may or may not be able to help you find it.

Types of Search Engines
There are many types of search engines. One such type is a search engine that is embedded in a website, e.g., the Library of Congress's website at http://www.loc.gov/ has a facility to search that site. This tool is useful when you know the site you want.

Some engines search within a specific subject e.g., Justia (http://www.justia.com/) for law or iMedisearch (http://www.imedisearch.com/) for medicine. In general, these subject directories are smaller and more selective than other search engines.

The most popular type of search engine is a universal search engine that tries to index the entire contents of the Internet, for example Google (http://www.google.com) or Bing (http://www.bing.com). A search in one of these search engines can return a huge number of 'hits' or results. When using one of these, it is best to develop a search strategy that will limit your search.

Other search engines allow searching for a specific type of media. For example, to search for information on maps, Google Maps (http://www.google.com/maps/) would be a good starting point. When searching for videos, a search on YouTube (http://www.youtube.com/) would be a logical beginning.

Online Portals
Online portals are sometimes referred to as web portals or digital gateways. A portal is a specifically designed website that provides an entry point to a range of information, tools and links found on the Internet. It is designed to be the starting point for users when they go online. It includes links to the most common types of information people look for (e.g., a general portal such as Yahoo! (http://yahoo.com) includes news, weather, entertainment and financial updates, as well as the facility to search the Internet). Portals may also be set up specifically for a particular industry, occupation or field of interest. The idea is that users will visit the portal as their first stop when searching for information.

EXERCISE 5.1

Answer the following questions.

1. Using the search facility located on the Library and Archives Canada site (http://www.collectionscanada.gc.ca/), find information about metadata.

2. Using the subject site for children's museums (http://www.childrensmuseums.org), find the location of the children's museum nearest you.

3. Using Google (http://www.google.com), Yahoo! (http://yahoo.com) and DuckDuckGo (http://duckduckgo.com/) compare the amount of information you can find on Davy Crockett.

Indexes and Directories

No matter which option you use to search the Internet, searching tools predominantly fall into two main categories: indexes, and directories. The differences between them are summarized in the following table.

	Indexes	**Directories**
Search options	• Only a search box appears	• Choices of different lists, topics and subjects • Offer the option to refine and search within specific categories
Results	• Links to large databases • Produced by web crawlers trawling through millions of web pages. • Not searching the Internet itself but the latest index produced by robot programs	• Sorts web pages for relevance using topics and categories
Advantages	• Most up-to-date form of searching • Delves deeper into cyberspace than directories	• Search results are more likely to be relevant • Links are sometimes censored • Some subject gateways concentrate their searching on specific areas on interest, which provides more relevant material than indexes
Disadvantages	• Search results often provide a long list of links • Index search will only return pages that exactly match your search terms • Cannot identify related topics • Many pages can't be indexed as they are invisible to robot programs	• Fewer pages included in the directory, so search is not as wide as index search • Pages are more likely to be out-of-date

Discovery Layers and Federated Searches

Discovery Layers

In simple terms, a discovery layer is a Google-like search across a library's resources. It allows library users to obtain search results from multiple library resources and view the results in a consistent format. It provides a single point of access to the library's collection across bought, licensed and digital materials. Its main aim is to connect users to the information they need as effortlessly as possible. Examples of discovery layers include: *Worldcat Local* by OCLC, *Summon* by Serials Solutions, *Primo Central* by Ex Libris, the *Ebsco Discovery Service* by

Ebsco and *Encore Synergy* by Innovative Interfaces. A discovery layer is also referred to as a: discovery service; web scale discovery service; resource discovery platform.

Discovery layers generally index databases, journal collections, library catalogs, institutional repositories and other collections. The discovery layer can therefore cover a far greater scope than a simple search of the library catalog.

Discovery layers only search the library resources that are available to the users at a particular institution. Therefore, users know that they will be able to access what they find, and the resources are accurate, current, and relevant for the clientele of that particular library. Discovery layers filter out many of the inaccurate or unobtainable results that can be retrieved when using a general search engine.

Federated Searches
Federated search allows the simultaneous searching of multiple searchable resources. A user conducts one search that is fed into the search engines and databases participating in the federation. The federated search then compiles the results that are received in one list for the user. Each search is conducted 'on the fly', so it takes longer than searching using tools that crawl and index items (such as search engine searches). However, using this process allows it to be a much lower maintenance system.

Federated search tools search databases and journal collections (but only those the library subscribes to), as well as the library's catalog. Examples of federated search tools include *WebFeat* by Serials Solutions and *MetaLib* by ExLibris.

Federated search tools are often used by smaller libraries, whose collections consist mainly of journal and e-book databases, journal collections, and resources contained in a single catalog.

Similarities Between Discovery Layers and Federated Searches
Discovery layers and federated searches:
- can be the starting point for research when the research needs are broad
- search and provide direct access to individual journal articles
- have customized content, as their tools default to searching resources owned by or accessible through the individual library
- include most journals in the library's collections
- offer basic as well as advanced searching
- indicate the database that articles come from
- offer additional features such as formatting and importing citations, and tagging
- have open source as well as commercial options.

Differences Between Discovery Layers and Federated Search
- Discovery layers search library catalogs, databases, institutional repositories and other collections. Federated search tools search library catalogs and databases.
- Discovery layers index and search, while federated search tools search 'on the fly'. This means that discovery layers will return results more quickly but require higher maintenance than federated searches.

Without the option to use a discovery layer or federated search, users have to conduct separate searches for different types of information (e.g., the library catalog for books and journals, databases for journal articles or individual e-journals, and other specialized databases). This can be a time-consuming exercise that involves duplicating the same search over and over in different places. Both discovery layers and federated searches offer a search box that allows searching across multiple resources, making it much easier to retrieve a variety of materials.

Websites

A website consists of one or more set of documents known as web pages that contain information (displayed using images, words, digital media, etc.). The main page in a website is called the home page, and other pages are called subpages. These are connected by hyperlinks that, when clicked, take the user to a different location (possibly another subpage, another location on the same page, or another website altogether).

Some websites require a subscription to access some or all of their content. Examples of websites include: business sites, parts of news websites, academic journal websites, gaming websites, file-sharing websites, message boards, web-based email, social networking websites, websites providing real-time stock market data.

Databases

A library database is a searchable electronic catalog or index that often contains information about published items. It usually requires an online subscription to access articles from sources such as magazines, newspapers, journals, and reference books. Some databases may also include videos, audio files, podcasts, blogs, and images.

Library databases provide citation information for the resources they list, including details such as: author, if available; title of article; publication details; publisher; date of publication. Some databases index items across many subject areas but most databases index materials from a specific focus or discipline.

A library catalog is an example of a database. It is a bibliographic database, that is, it provides a descriptive record of the library's resources, but the resources themselves are not provided in the database. While the library catalog lists the titles of journals that are available, most library catalogs do not list individual articles from the library's journal holdings. To locate journal articles on a specific topic or by a particular author, you need to use one of the types of databases explained below.

Types of Databases

Databases are divided into four types, depending on the content they provide: bibliographic, full-text, a combination of both, or content specific databases.

Bibliographic Databases
Bibliographic databases provide a citation (and usually an abstract) for each resource that is included in the database. They do not provide direct access to the full-text of the journal articles they cite.

Full-text Databases
Full-text databases provide access to the complete text of articles and documents. Some of them, however, contain only the publications of one publisher and not a comprehensive overview of what has been published on a topic. For example:
- *Science Direct* (only Elsevier publications)
- *Wiley Interscience* (only Blackwell/Wiley publications)
- *SpringerLink* (only Springer/Kluwer publications).

Combination Databases
Combination databases are usually multidisciplinary covering a range of subject areas. They include content from different publishers, and the content provided is determined by the arrangements made with individual publishers. Consequently, search results in combination databases will include a mixture of journal article citations (and abstracts) as well as full-text journal articles.

Content Specific Databases
Content specific databases provide information that covers particular subjects, such as financial and market data like annual reports, company information, country information, and investor reports.

Types of Database Searches
Before beginning to search in any database, you will need to identify the best terms to use for retrieving information about your topic. There are two ways that searches can be done:
- keyword searching
- subject searching.

Keyword searching, as the name suggests, use natural language in the search strategy. It is necessary to decide what are the important words or phrases relevant to the topic. Then, type these keywords into the search box in any order and retrieve records that contain those search terms.

This type of searching is an option in most databases, library catalogs and library networks, e.g., *Trove* and *WorldCat*. It is also the way that most searches are conducted on the Internet.

Subject searching involves searching the subject headings that have been assigned to each item in a database. By searching these headings you are able to find relevant items on the same topic. To find subject headings for a topic, see if the database has an online or published thesaurus to browse for subjects that match the topic. This information is usually available on the Help screens.

It is not always clear whether to start with a subject search or a keyword search. Sometimes the results of one type of search are better than the other, and sometimes it might be more appropriate to conduct both types of searches in order to find all the information that is needed.

Understanding the differences between keyword searching and subject searching will help to improve searching techniques. Here are some of the key differences:

	Keyword	**Subject**
What it is	<ul><li>A keyword search looks in any field</li><li>Uses natural language or uncontrolled vocabulary</li><li>Reflects current usage (without being prescribed) and is the language found in the documents</li></ul>	<ul><li>A subject search looks only in the subject field</li><li>Uses prescribed language or controlled vocabulary (e.g., LCSH, or database defined terms)</li><li>Prescribed subject headings reflect a careful selection of terminology so as to avoid the scattering of related subjects under different headings</li></ul>
When to use it	<ul><li>When controlled vocabulary is not known</li><li>When you want to find the subject heading by using a keyword</li><li>When no subject heading exists to describe your topic (too new, etc.)</li><li>When you have several different concepts to apply to one search</li></ul>	<ul><li>When controlled vocabulary is known</li><li>When too much material is retrieved by a keyword search</li><li>When specialist vocabulary is needed (e.g., MeSH)</li></ul>
Advantages	<ul><li>Provides access to new terms or topics that may not yet be reflected in controlled vocabulary</li><li>Usually results in a broader search, therefore it is more likely to retrieve something</li><li>Provides access to subject headings 'accidentally'</li></ul>	<ul><li>Provides one authoritative heading for a particular subject, regardless of how many different keywords are related to the topic</li><li>Results in a more orderly search, often including access to related, broader and narrower terms</li></ul>
Disadvantages	<ul><li>Too many hits</li><li>False hits</li><li>Not necessarily comprehensive</li></ul>	<ul><li>May not reflect current usage resulting in unsuccessful searches, especially for very current topics</li><li>Impossible to retrieve hits if not using proper subject headings</li></ul>

ACTIVITY 5.2

Select a database that you can access either at your library, or your local public library. Choose a topic that interests you and search using the steps listed below.

1. Conduct a keyword search, using the important words or phrases that best describe your topic.

2. Browse the results list and choose 2 or 3 articles that are relevant to your topic.

3. Look at the subject headings that have been used for these items.

4. Conduct your search again, using those subject headings.

5. Look at your results for the subject search and compare these results with those from your initial keyword search. (They should be more precise than your initial keyword search.)

Differences Between Databases and Websites

Even though databases and websites are all accessed on the Internet there are some key differences between them. The table below outlines a number of these differences.

	Databases	Websites
Authority	Easy to determine. Most databases have a scholarly/peer-reviewed filter or contain only scholarly literature. Authority and trustworthiness are almost guaranteed.	Varies and difficult to verify. Cannot limit to professional, scholarly literature. Information on websites is seldom regulated, which means authority is often in doubt.
Number of Hits	Dozens to hundreds of hits - a more manageable number, and duplicates can be filtered out.	Thousands, sometimes millions, of hits, much of the same information is repackaged or duplicated. Duplicates are not filtered out.
Relevance	Focus by subject (e.g., business, art, medicine) and/or format (e.g., journals, books, book reviews), which often means more relevant information and less time wasted dealing with junk. Information comes from legitimate, quality controlled sources.	Lack of subject focus, unless you are using a subject-specific search engine, can result in numerous irrelevant hits. Much information on websites is opinionated and biased. Quantity doesn't equal quality.
Search Features	Numerous advanced search features determined by database (e.g., limiting by publication type, date, language, document format, scholarly/peer-reviewed status).	Vary between search engines, but often restricted. Can limit by document type (.doc, .pdf) or language, but limiting by publication date, format, and scholarly/peer-reviewed is often not available.
Access to Public Information	Databases deal only with published information (i.e., information that originally appeared in print: magazine and journal articles, books, etc.) They are more stable than the Web. Accessed for free through a subscription service that the library pays for.	Website information often lives and dies on the Internet and can come from anyone with Internet access. Much information does not come from legitimate published sources: magazines, academic journals, books, etc. When it is, the user usually has to pay to access it.
Currency	Updated frequently and include the date of publication.	May not contain current information or indicate when a page is updated.

EXERCISE 5.3

Identify which of the following search requests could be conducted using the Internet and which ones will require you to access a database.

1. How to fill in tax forms

2. Article from a peer-reviewed journal

3. A specific website

4. Information on a new topic

5. Biographical information

6. Statistical information

Search Functions

Most search engines have both basic and advanced search functions. Many of these search functions are used when searching websites and databases.

Basic Search Features

While individual search engines and databases may have their own unique features, in general the following basic rules apply when searching.

- **Capitalization** doesn't matter (e.g., 'United States of America' and 'united states of america' are considered to be the same search).

- **Order**. Most search engines and databases search for all the words in your search in any order (e.g., if you type in new zealand sky tower, the search engine will look for all of the pages with the word new, the word Zealand, the word sky and the word tower anywhere in the page but not necessarily in that order).

- **Quotation marks** can be used to make most search engines and databases search for a phrase as a single unit (e.g., typing "new zealand sky tower" will retrieve pages that discuss the New Zealand Sky Tower as a single unit rather than the separate words in the search).

- **Stop words** are not searched by most search engines or databases. These are 'insignificant' words that appear in a database record or web page. Common stop words include: a, an, the, in, of, on, are, be, if, into, which. However, stop words can vary in different databases. Check the 'Help' screens for the relevant list of stop words for the database or search engine.

Advanced Search Features

Using the advanced search option allows you to conduct a more focused search, and narrows the number of hits. Techniques that can make a search more precise are outlined below. Not all of these techniques work in every search engine or database, so checking the 'Help' link in the search engine or database for more information is beneficial.

- **Boolean Operators**: are connecting words placed between search terms to narrow or expand a search.
  - AND: Helps to Narrow a Search = It tells the computer that both terms must be present in the record (e.g., fruit AND vegetables).
  - OR: Helps to Broaden a Search = It is used for like or synonymous terms. Using it tells the computer that either term must be present in the record (e.g., fruit OR vegetables).
  - NOT: Helps to Narrow a Search = It eliminates an unwanted search term or group of search terms from the search results (e.g., fruit NOT vegetables).

- **Truncation**: broadens your search to take into account plurals, various word endings and spellings. To use truncation, enter the root of a word and put the truncation symbol at the end. The database will return results that include any ending of that root word (e.g., child* = child, childs, children, childrens, childhood). Truncation symbols may vary by database but common symbols include: *, !, ?, or #.

- **Wildcards**: substitute a symbol for one letter of a word. This allows you to adjust for variations in spelling within a word (e.g., wom?n = woman, women or defen?e = defense, defence). Not all search systems allow wildcard searching but for those that do, '?' is the most common wildcard symbol.

- **Phrase Searching**: Most databases allow you to specify that adjacent words be searched as phrases. Using parentheses or double quotes around search words is a common way to do phrase searching (e.g., "global financial crisis") but not all databases or search engines use them.

- **Proximity Operators**: Many databases allow you to specify that the words you are searching are close to each other in the record or document. The proximity operators vary according to the database, but some common ones include:
  - 'w#' = with. It specifies that words appear in the order you type them in. Substitute the # with the number of words that may appear in between the words (e.g., 'tax w3 reform' tells the computer 'tax' and 'reform' must appear in this order in a document, but can be up to 3 words apart).

- ○ 'n#' = near. It specifies that the words may appear in any order. Substitute the # with a number of words that may appear in between the words. (e.g., 'tax n3 reform' tells the computer 'tax' and 'reform' can appear in any order in a document, and be up to 3 words apart).

- **Nesting**: with a complicated search, you can put the various parts in parentheses, to make it easier for the computer to understand. This is useful when you are mixing ANDs and ORs (e.g., (fruit OR vegetables) AND (cereals OR grains)).

- **Fields**: contain specific pieces of bibliographic information in library databases. Common fields include: author, title, journal title, abstract, publisher, date of publication and subject. Limiting your search to specific fields can yield more precise results. To find various fields within a database, look for drop down boxes or menus to select the field you want to search. Then combine words and fields together with Boolean or proximity operators for a more precise search.

- **Limiting**: is another way to make your results more specific. Many of the same Field options (discussed above) are able to be used as limits, however, limit options will vary between databases. For example, you may only want to retrieve full-text articles or limit your results to articles published in certain years.

- **Searching for Information from a Specific Site**: if you need information from a specific site, you can limit the search to a type of site (e.g., .edu or .gov) or to a specific domain (e.g., edu.ph). You do this by using the term 'site:' in the search (e.g., history AND site:edu.ph). This works in Google and some, but not all, other search engines.

Relevance Sorting

The results of a completed search need to be looked at to select the information that will be most relevant. Search engines and databases rank the results using some of the following criteria to determine relevance:

- **Proximity**: how close the search terms are.

- **Frequency**: a page that has the term(s) mentioned a lot will rank higher than pages that mention it only once or twice.

- **Completeness**: for search engines that do not require every term to appear, pages with all of the terms will rank higher than pages with only some of them.

- **Locations**: most search engines can tell where the terms appear and increase the rank of a page with the terms in the title or section headings above pages where the terms just appear in the body.

- **Links**: some search engines examine the links to the page to increase the rank of pages that have more links from similar pages.

- **Date**: databases will often present resources in chronological order—sometimes by the date published but sometimes according to the date they were added to the database.

While you may not be able to determine which of these relevance criteria your search engine or database is using, it is important to realize that something is happening in the background. You might like to try similar searches using more than one search engine to see if one ranks resources that are useful to you in a different order from another search engine.

Use the 'Help' screens to find out how to combine search terms, what truncation and wildcard symbols to use, and what other search features are available on that database.

Tips for Searching
1. **Plan your search strategy**
   Make sure you understand what kind of information you require. Select the concepts and then identify keywords or subject terms that will describe them.

2. **Select your database**
   Select the most relevant database/s for your search.

3. **Perform your database search**
   Search the database using your concepts, keywords or subject terms.

4. **Evaluate the results**
   Look at your search results. Look at the citation abstracts and subject headings. Are they relevant? Identify those citations that will be useful.

5. **Do you have too many results?**
   Check your use of OR and AND.
   Use the database filtering options. For instance do you need a particular publication type, or specific date range?

6. **Do you have too few results?**
   Try adding other search terms and combinations.
   Have you found recurring subject headings that you could use?
   Are there more synonyms for your keywords?
   Use truncation or wildcard features.
   You may need to edit your search several times to retrieve the most relevant citations.
   If you have expanded the search as far as you can and are still not getting enough results, try searching on another database in the subject area.

7. **Save the search results**
   Use print, email, save or export options.

8. **Locate the full-text**
   If you are searching a full-text database, click on the link to get to the article.
   If the database doesn't contain full-text articles, take a note of the citation and search to see if you are able to access the article elsewhere. It may be necessary to check print journals or ask for an article on interlibrary loan.

Refine your results
After you have completed your search, if you did not find relevant results or need to find more, you should:
- check your spelling
- consider using alternative keywords/subjects e.g., use 'sweets' or 'lollies' as well as 'candy'
- use alternative spellings such as 'organization' OR 'organisation'
- use truncation symbols or wildcards to capture all forms of your keywords
- check that you have used Boolean operators correctly
- search other databases.

If you found too many references, you could narrow your search or make it more specific:
- add another concept and associated keywords
- restrict your search to specific fields such as 'abstract'
- add search limiters to your search such as 'date range' or 'peer reviewed'.

After conducting your searches, display the search results and evaluate them to see if they match your topic.

REVISION QUIZ 5.4
Use the following questions to revise your understanding of searching for electronic information. You do not need to write down the answers.

1. Define online portals.

2. What similarities are there between discovery layers and federated searches?

3. Explain the differences between keyword searches and subject searches.

4. What are five advanced search features you could use when searching in databases?

5. Name five ways that you could refine your results.

CHAPTER SIX
Social Media and Information

Introduction
People have always loved to share their views on the best restaurants in town, their latest fashion tips or where to go for the next vacation. This is the kind of information that is often shared in conversations between friends. Using the Internet, and with the evolution of new technologies, passing on social information has become even easier. Web pages that are known as Web 2.0 sites allow users to interact with one another in dialog, using social media tools. These sites are in contrast with traditional websites that are limited to the passive viewing of content on web pages. Some examples of Web 2.0 sites are social networking sites, blogs, wikis, folksonomies, and video sharing sites.

What is Social Media?
Online social tools, known as social media, encourage communication and facilitate opportunities to gather information, share stories and discuss concerns between individuals, corporations, and organizations.

Social media is a catch-all term used to describe a variety of Internet applications that allow users to create and share content, thus interacting with each other. This interaction can take many forms, but common types include:
- sharing links to interesting content produced by third parties
- public updates to a profile where someone describes him/herself, 'posts' a summary of their personal details, information on current activities or even location data
- sharing photos, videos and posts
- commenting on photos, posts, updates, videos and links shared by others.

Social media can be a powerful tool to distribute information. One of its most innovative aspects is that it has the capacity to deliver free information instantaneously. Content that is shared via social media has the potential to be sent to one single person or up to millions of people, depending on its reach, its message, and its intended audience. It allows anyone to publish and deliver news, information, or other resources, which means that anyone with access to the Internet can be a content creator.

Different Types of Social Media
In general, social media can be grouped into six categories according to their ability to provide certain social functions:
- social networks
- bookmarking sites
- social news
- media sharing

- microblogging
- blog comments and forums.

Each of these categories contains its own set of characteristics.

Social Networks
Social networks allow you to connect with other people of similar interests and background. They usually consist of a profile, various ways to interact with other users, and the ability to set up groups, etc. The most popular social networks are Facebook and LinkedIn.

Bookmarking Sites
Bookmarking sites, also known as folksonomies, allow you to save, organize and manage links to various websites and online resources. Most bookmarking sites allow you to 'tag' your links to make them easy to search and share. The most popular of these sites are Pinterest and Delicious.

Social News
Social news allows people to post news items or links to outside articles. Users then 'vote' on the items and those items with the highest number of votes are displayed most prominently. The community therefore decides which news items will be seen by more people. The most popular social news sites are Digg and Reddit.

Media Sharing
Media sharing allows you to upload and share various media such as pictures and video. Most media sharing services have additional social features such as the ability to create profiles, and the option of commenting on uploaded content. The most popular of these sites are YouTube and Flickr.

Microblogging
Microblogging allows users to submit short written entries that may include links to product and service sites, as well as links to other social media sites. These entries are then posted to everyone who has subscribed to that user's account. The most popular microblogging website is Twitter.

Blog Comments and Forums
Blog comments and forums allow members to hold conversations by posting and responding to messages. Blog comments are attached to blogs where the discussion centers around the topic of the blog post. There are many popular blogs and forums.

You will notice that although social media can be broken down into these six different categories, there is some overlap between the various services. For example, Facebook has microblogging features with its 'status update'. Flickr and YouTube also have comment facilities similar to that of blogs.

Examples of Social Media

There are an enormous number of social media sites available. The table below provides brief details about some of the more popular social media tools.

Social Media Site & URL	Description
Facebook http://www.facebook.com	Facebook is a free social networking website that allows registered users to create profiles, upload photos and video, send messages and keep in touch with others who have created their own Facebook profile. Unlike email or instant messaging, which are usually private exchanges, the information you post on Facebook is public. However, Facebook does offer privacy tools to allow you to limit who can see what you share. It is designed to be more open and social than traditional communication tools.
Twitter http://www.twitter.com	Twitter is a free social messaging service for sending and receiving short messages in real time. Messages are limited to 140 characters called 'tweets'. Registered users can read and post tweets, but unregistered users can only read them without forwarding or commenting on them. Twitter is also an online social networking service because if offers the facility for people to create their own profile and connect with others online.
LinkedIn http://www.linkedin.com	LinkedIn is a free business-oriented social networking service that is mostly used for professional networking. It allows users to create profiles and connections to each other in an online social network that may represent professional relationships. Users can invite anyone else to become a connection, even if they are not yet on LinkedIn. This is one of the ways that LinkedIn expands its network.
Instagram http://instagram.com	Instagram is an online mobile photo-sharing, video-sharing and social networking service that enables its users to take pictures and videos, and share them on a variety of social networking platforms.
Pinterest http://www.pinterest.com	Pinterest is a storage tool that allows users to create and share the collections of visual bookmarks, or boards, that they gather. Boards are created when a user selects an item, page, website, etc., and pins it to an existing or newly created board. Users save and share these pins from multiple resources onto boards for their own viewing and for others to see as well. Pinterest is used as a digital bulletin board or a scrapbook for collecting the things you find online.

Tumblr http://www.tumblr.com/	Tumblr allows users to post multimedia and other content (including text, photos, quotes, links, chat, audio and video) to a short-form blog. It is possible to follow other users' blogs, as well as make your own blog private. The website's features are accessed from the 'dashboard' interface, where the option to post content and posts of followed blogs appear.
YouTube http://www.youtube.com	YouTube is a free video-sharing website that allows users to upload, view, and share videos. It displays a wide variety of user-generated videos as well as corporate media video. Available content includes video clips, TV clips, music videos, and other content such as video blogging, short original videos, and educational videos. Unregistered users can watch videos, while registered users can upload videos to their channels.
Wikipedia http://www.wikipedia.org	Wikipedia is a freely accessible Internet encyclopedia. Entries are created in a collaborative effort by a community of users known as Wikipedians. Anyone registered on the site can create an article for publication. There are, however, restrictions placed on those entries that are sensitive or vandalism-prone so they are protected to some degree.
Flickr http://www.flickr.com/	Flickr is a free photo sharing site that does not compress the size of images but stores and displays them at full resolution. It offers users one terabyte of storage for their photos and short videos. It also provides a range of basic photo-editing tools. Users can not only store, sort and search their photos, but they can easily share their Flickr photos back to other social media sites.

Generally, social media sites focus on a particular type of social engagement. For example, those using Facebook are mainly interested in conversations, connections, and sharing between individuals and organizations, so Facebook is structured to make this kind of activity as easy as possible. Those using LinkedIn are more professionally oriented, focusing on business relationships, branding, and job-related information, so its structure makes relationships less casual and more businesslike. Twitter users enjoy sharing, conversing with other users, becoming part of a larger group, and building reputation, so Twitter's structure is built to enhance these goals.

EXERCISE 6.1

There are many more social media sites apart from the examples listed above. Find four more sites and provide the URL and some brief information about each one.

Social Media Site & URL	Description

Functions of Social Media

Social media may also be grouped according to the functions performed by specific tools. They can be broken down into the following seven functional building blocks:
- identity
- conversations
- sharing
- presence
- relationships
- reputation
- groups.

Different social media activities are defined by the extent to which they focus on some or all of these building blocks, as explained below.

Identity
The extent to which users reveal their identities in a social media setting is represented in this building block. It can include disclosing information such as name, age, gender, profession, location, and any other information that portrays users in certain ways.

Conversations
Many social media sites are designed primarily to facilitate conversations among individuals and groups. This block represents the extent to which users communicate with other users in a social media setting. These conversations happen for all sorts of reasons. People tweet, blog, etc., to meet new like-minded people, to find companionship, to build their self-esteem, or to be on the cutting edge of new ideas or trending topics. Others see social media as a way of making their message heard and positively impacting humanitarian causes, environmental problems, economic issues, or political debates.

Sharing
This block represents the extent to which users exchange, distribute, and receive content. The term 'social' often implies that exchanges between people are crucial. In many cases, however, the social element is really about why they meet online and associate with each other.

Presence
The extent to which users can know if other users are accessible is determined by presence. It includes knowing where others are, in the virtual world and/or in the real world, and whether they are available to interact.

Relationships
This block represents the extent to which users can relate to other users. Two or more users have some form of association that leads them to converse, share socially, meet up, or simply list each other as a friend or fan.

Reputation
Reputation can have different meanings on social media platforms. This block represents the extent to which users can identify the standing of others, including themselves, in a social

media setting. In most cases, reputation is a matter of trust, but because information technologies are not good at determining such highly qualitative criteria, social media sites rely on tools that automatically aggregate user-generated information to determine trustworthiness.

Groups

The extent to which users can form communities and subcommunities is represented by groups. The more 'social' a network becomes, the bigger the group of friends, followers, and contacts.

EXERCISE 6.2

Identify three social networks that are examples of each of the seven functional building blocks of social media listed above.

	Example 1	Example 2	Example 3
Identity			
Conversations			
Sharing			
Presence			
Relationships			
Reputation			
Groups			

Using Social Media Safely

It is wise when using social media to follow some best practices such as those that follow.
- Ensure you have effective and updated antivirus/antispyware software and a firewall running before you go online.
- Do not allow peer pressure to convince you to do something you are not comfortable with.
- Be wary of publishing any identifying information about yourself—either in your profile or in your posts—such as phone numbers, pictures of your home, or your address.
- Use a strong password that cannot easily be hacked.
- Keep your profile closed and allow only your friends to view your profile.
- Do not say anything or publish pictures that might later cause you or someone else embarrassment, as once something is online it stays online.
- Never post comments that may cause offense to any individual, group or organization.
- Be aware of what friends post about you, or how they reply to your posts, particularly regarding your personal details and activities.
- Be careful about what you say, what pictures you post, and how you present yourself in your profile, as many companies routinely view current or prospective employees' social media pages.
- Use the privacy features of the social media site to restrict strangers' access to your profile, thus being guarded about who you let join your network.
- Be careful of phishing scams, including fake friend requests and posts from individuals or companies inviting you to visit other pages or sites.
- If you do get caught in a scam, make sure you remove any corresponding likes and permissions from your account.

Benefits of Social Media

While there are risks involved in using online social media, there are many potential benefits for those engaged in social media. Social networking can provide opportunities to develop new relationships as well as strengthening existing relationships. It can make and maintain social connections and support networks that otherwise would not be possible. The communities and social interactions people form online can be invaluable in helping them bolster and develop self-confidence and social skills.

People tend to use social networking to add to, not replace, their real-world relationships, helping them learn to communicate in different ways. Social networking is an increasingly important method of communicating in the workplace, to assist in the sharing of information, opinion and discussion.

The use of social media and networking services such as Facebook, Twitter, and Instagram have become an integral part of the daily lives of many people. Some of the positive benefits of social media include:
- social participation
- learning social skills
- creating, managing and distributing content

- exploring and learning
- developing new skills.

Social Participation
Social networking services can provide an accessible toolkit for highlighting and acting on issues and causes that affect and interest people. Social media can be used for organizing activities, events, or groups to showcase issues and opinions and make a wider audience aware of them (e.g., coordinating fundraisers, or creating awareness of various causes).

Learning Social Skills
Social media can help users discover public ways of presenting themselves. Personal skills are very important in this context: to make, develop and keep friendships, and to be regarded as a trusted connection within a network. Social media can provide opportunities to learn how to function successfully in a community, navigate a public social space and learn social norms and skills as participants in peer groups.

Creating, Managing and Distributing Content
Users can take part in activities and discussions on a site, and upload, modify or create content. This encourages creativity and can support discussion about the ownership of content and managing this data. People who use social networking services to showcase content (e.g., music, film, photography or writing) need to know what permissions they are giving the host service, so that they can make informed decisions about how and what they place on the site. Users might also want to explore additional licensing options that may be available to them within services (e.g., Creative Commons licensing) to allow them to share their work with other people in a range of ways.

Exploring and Learning
Social networks encourage discovery. If someone is interested in certain books, recipes or ideas, it is likely that their interest will be catered for by a social networking service or group within a service. If users are looking for something more specific or unusual they could create their own groups or social networking sites. Social networking services can help people develop their interests and find other people who share the same interests. They can help introduce people to new concepts and ideas, and deepen appreciation of existing interests. They can also help broaden users' horizons by helping them discover how other people live and think in other parts of the world.

Developing New Skills
Managing an online presence and being able to interact effectively online is becoming an increasingly important skill in the workplace. Being able to adapt quickly to new technologies, services and environments is regarded by employers as a highly valuable skill and can facilitate both formal and informal learning. Most services are text-based, which encourages literacy skills, including interpretation, evaluation and contextualization.

Social Media as an Information Source

Although social media was primarily designed as a social tool, it has caused a change in the way that information is sought. People, especially younger people, are engaging in social media sites rather than traditional websites for all kinds of information, and frequently using these sites as their 'first port of call' for information. Students, in particular, are increasingly turning to Web 2.0 sites for their information needs (e.g., Wikipedia and YouTube). The pages retrieved in their Google search may well include blogs or posted questions and answers in their search results, along with more traditional information. It is imperative, therefore, that information agencies are accessible, where their users are, to connect with them for their information seeking. This may mean that libraries need to reinvent some of what they do to meet the information needs of their clients.

A large percentage of libraries and information agencies have accounts on a range of social media (e.g., the New York Public Library has accounts on Facebook, Twitter, Instagram, Tumblr, Flickr, Yelp)—with library staff posting messages on social media daily. Libraries and information agencies use social media, primarily to promote their services and resources. They may allow feedback from clients, or provide a reference service using social media (e.g., via Facebook or Twitter). Social media is also used as a collection management tool that offers varying ways to present resources (e.g. YouTube for video delivery).

Libraries and information agencies take up opportunities to use social media in order to:
- take the library service to users in their preferred spaces
- build a sense of community between the library and its users
- take advantage of the low costs involved with using social media.

While there are benefits to accessing information from a range of sources, concerns have been raised about the quality and credibility of the information found on social media. It can be difficult to assess what is available through social media as it has been created and shared by users, and is not filtered through a mediation process. It is perhaps more important to evaluate social media sites than other information sources. Chapter 3 of this workbook provides criteria for evaluating social media sites.

REVISION QUIZ 6.3

Use the following questions to revise your understanding of social media. You do not need to write down the answers.

1. Define social media.

2. What are the seven functions of social media outlined in this workbook?

3. What five steps could you take to use social media safely?

4. List three benefits of using social media.

CHAPTER SEVEN
Bibliographic Elements

Introduction

In Chapter 4 we considered different types of information packages. The information industry, particularly libraries and publishers, describes these information packages in terms of their bibliographic elements (author, title, publisher, place of publication, etc.) and their physical format.

When working in a library or other information agency you need to be able to identify these elements in a range of information packages. Bibliographic elements are also important when preparing a bibliography or a catalog entry for an item.

Elements of Bibliographic Records

Bibliographic elements are stored in a bibliographic record that usually consists of the following data:

element name	element content
author	who is responsible for the intellectual or artistic content
title	what the resource is called
publication statement	where, by whom and when was it published
copyright date	when copyright was asserted for the resource
edition	a particular form or version of a published resource, often numbered
format	the physical packaging of the content, such as a printed book
physical characteristics	the number and type of units, such as number of pages
standard number(s)	registered numbers such as ISBN
subject	what is the resource about

The bibliographic record helps library users decide whether the resource described in the record is the one they require or whether it contains the information they want.

Exercise 7.1

Examine the title and verso pages of this workbook. Write down the following information and where you found it.

1. Who is the author?

2. What is the title of the book?

3. Is there a subtitle? What is it?

4. Where was the book published?

5. Who is the publisher?

6. When was this edition published?

7. Is the book part of a series?

8. What is the ISBN?

9. Is there a dedication?

10. Does the book include an index?

11. Does the book have a glossary?

12. Does the book have a bibliography?

EXERCISE 7.2

Examine a serial. Write down the following information and where you found it. Some of the information may be on the title and verso pages but other information may be harder to find. Check areas like the cover, back cover or contents page.

1. What is the title of the serial?

2. Where is the serial published?

3. Who publishes the serial?

4. What is the publisher's address?

5. How often is the serial published?

6. What is the volume number?

7. What is the issue number?

8. What is the date of the issue?

9. What is the ISSN for the serial?

10. Does the serial have a title page as well as a cover?

11. Does the title page (or cover) include a table of contents?

12. How much does a subscription cost?

Exercise 7.3

Examine a non-book item carefully. Write down the following information and where you found it. Answer only the questions that apply to your item.

1. What is the physical format of the item?

2. What is the title?

3. Who is the creator (author, composer, scriptwriter, etc)?

4. Who published the resource?

5. Is it distributed by an organization other than the publisher?

6. Where was it originally published?

7. When was it originally published?

8. Who produced the resource?

9. List the performers:

10. What are its dimensions?

11. What is the playing time?

12. What equipment does it need to access the information?

EXERCISE 7.4

Examine a website. Write down the following information and where you found it. Some of the information may be hard to find on the main pages of the website.

1. What is the title of the website?

2. Is there an author mentioned, or a sponsoring organization?

3. Is a date given for the last update?

4. Is there a site map on the website?

5. Does this website include copyright information? Where is it located?

EXERCISE 7.5

Having examined a monograph, a serial, a non-book item and a website, note the similarities and the differences between the packages. Add to the list if you can.

Does the item have:	Monograph	Serial	Non-book item	Website
author				
title				
publisher				
place of publication				
date of publication				
page numbers				
index				
duration				
illustrations				
frequency statement				
price				
contents table				
erasure tabs				
dust jacket				

The Catalog

A catalog is a systematically arranged record of the resources that are located in a collection, a library or a group of libraries. As the catalog provides full bibliographic information for each resource held in the collection, it is the most efficient way to find resources. When you search the catalog, the bibliographic record tells you where the resources are located and whether physical resources are currently in the library or out on loan.

The purposes of the catalog, as determined by the International Federation of Library Associations and Institutions (IFLA) are to:
- **Find** - locate a resource in a database or catalog when a user searches on one or more of its characteristics, e.g., title
- **Identify** – use the descriptive data to confirm that the resource found is the one that was wanted, or to distinguish between resources with similar characteristics (e.g., two works with the same title)
- **Select** – choose the resource that meets the user's needs regarding its format and content (e.g., a DVD rather than a videocassette, or a text in a specific language)
- **Obtain** – acquire or access the resource by borrowing it, buying it or connecting to it online, etc.

Cataloging

Cataloging is the process of creating bibliographic records to describe the resources held in a collection. These records are located in the library's catalog, usually referred to as the OPAC (**O**nline **P**ublic **A**ccess **C**atalog).

The cataloging process includes:
- descriptive cataloging
- subject cataloging
- classification.

Catalogers use a range of tools to determine the information that is useful to include in a bibliographic record. They gather the bibliographic information using established standardized instructions, which allow libraries to share their records.

Descriptive Cataloging

Descriptive cataloging describes a resource so that it can be identified. Its purpose is to give sufficient information to the user to help them select the required item. The instruction set used for descriptive cataloging is *Resource description and access (RDA)*, which replaces *Anglo-American cataloguing rules second edition (AACR2)*. It is important to use standard instructions to describe the item and to determine access points.

EXERCISE 7.6
Using dictionaries, glossaries and your own knowledge, write definitions for each of the following cataloging terms.

Access point

Authority file

Authorized access point

Book number

Call number

Classification number

Subject heading

Variant access point

Subject Cataloging
Subject cataloging describes the content of a resource using subject headings and a classification number. Subject headings are determined using *Library of Congress subject headings (LCSH)* or a similar authoritative subject headings list.

Subject Headings
It is important that library staff use a standard list of subject headings, such as the *Library of Congress subject headings (LCSH)*, to ensure uniformity. Users also need guidance from headings which are not used to those that are used.

EXERCISE 7.7

Find the answers to the following questions using the Library of Congress subject headings (http://authorities.loc.gov).

1. Are the following terms acceptable as subject headings?
   a. 'Stand-up comedy'

   b. 'Earthmovers'

   c. 'Crops – Ecology'

   d. 'Meat-eating animals'

2. What types of publications would you include under the subject heading 'Collectibles'?

3. 'Community and school' is an accepted term in LCSH but 'Community and libraries' is not. What term would you use instead?

4. Is there a scope note under the term 'Psychological warfare'?

5. Would I find any information in a library catalog under the subject heading 'Chinaware'?

6. I found some information on 'Wedding etiquette' in the catalog. Can you suggest some broader subject headings that would lead me to more information?

Classification

Classification is a system for arranging library resources according to their subject. The classification number provides a shelving location for a resource in a physical collection. It assists the user to find an item when the call number is known, and to find all items of one kind together.

Materials may be classified:
- by format (e.g., monographs, folios, serials, reference, audiovisual, fiction, non-fiction, large-print)
- by use (e.g., children, adults, foreign language)
- by subject or topic.

Most libraries rely on a classification system based on subject, as well as a mixture of classification by use or format.

Classification schemes used today are recognized systems. Their arrangements and notations are widely known and understood. For example Dewey Decimal Classification and Library of Congress Classification are widely used by libraries and bibliographic services.

Dewey Decimal Classification

The Dewey Decimal Classification system (DDC) was created by Melvil Dewey in 1876 to "organize all knowledge". DDC divides knowledge into ten main classes. As it is a hierarchical system, within each broad class, it develops progressively from the general to the specific (i.e., each main class is divided into ten divisions, and each division into ten sections). DDC uses a minimum of three digits, followed by a decimal point and further digits as necessary.

This is the world's most widely used classification scheme. It is used most often in public and school libraries. Many libraries use DDC because:
- the decimal notation is simple to assign, shelve, remember and find
- the scheme is revised periodically to accommodate new topics
- widespread use of DDC and computer technology make it possible for libraries to share the work of classifying.

Library of Congress Classification

The Library of Congress Classification system was developed by the Library of Congress to organize its own collection. It has been adopted by many libraries throughout the world, particularly large academic and special libraries. This classification scheme divides knowledge into twenty-one broad disciplines, each identified by a single letter of the alphabet. Each main class is further divided into subclasses by using additional letters; and numbers are used for divisions.

There are over forty printed volumes in the series (which are referred to as schedules), each with its own index. New classifications are devised when new subjects are added to the collection at the Library of Congress. Gaps are left in the schedules to provide for further inclusions.

Universal Decimal Classification

The Universal Decimal Classification system is based on Dewey Decimal Classification and was first published in 1905. It was developed by the International Federation for Information and Documentation (FID), an international organization created to promote universal access to all recorded knowledge.

This classification scheme seeks to cover all knowledge and to be international. It was originally designed as an indexing and retrieval system and is used mainly in special libraries and in specialized published bibliographies. The basic notation uses decimal numbers as in DDC, but the notation can be expanded by the use of a decimal point or other device such as a colon or bracket after each concept, e.g., Mathematical geology in Japan - 53:551(52).

EXERCISE 7.8

Answer the following questions about DDC.

1. Find the meaning for the following DDC hierarchical progressions using *Dewey decimal classification* volumes 2 and 3 (Schedules). (That is, take each Dewey number and build on it to get to the final Dewey call number).

    a. 000
       060
       069
       069.1
       069.13
       069.132

    b. 300
       340
       341
       341.4
       341.48

    c. 500
       540
       541
       541.2
       541.24

    d. 600
       610
       612
       612.1
       612.13
       612.133

e. 700
   740
   741
   741.5
   741.58

2. Find DDC numbers for the following subjects using Volume 4 (Relative Index) and the schedules of *Dewey decimal classification*.
   When classifying by DDC, note that the Relative Index is a guide to the scheme. Use it to find numbers, and then always check them in the schedules.

Elephants

Jackals

Farming

Library science

EXERCISE 7.9

Answer the following questions about LCC.

1. Each main class of LCC has subclasses. Below is a list of the subclasses for the main class H.

H	Social Sciences (General)
HA	Statistics
HB	Economic Theory. Demography
HC	Economic History and Conditions
HD	Industries. Land Use. Labor
HE	Transportation and Communications
HF	Commerce
HG	Finance
HJ	Public Finance
HM	Sociology (General)
HN	Social History and Conditions. Social Problems. Social Reform
HQ	The Family. Marriage. Women
HS	Societies: Secret, Benevolent, etc.
HT	Communities. Classes. Races
HV	Social Pathology. Social and Public Welfare. Criminology
HX	Socialism. Communism. Utopias. Anarchism

Using this list, write down the subclass to which each of the following topics belongs (i.e., which 2 letter code would you use).

a. World banking

b. The future of speed rail

c. Encyclopedia of sociology

d. Readings on international trade

e. The caste system in India

f. Government income and expenditure

2. Browse the LCC schedule at QH540 Ecology – either online (e.g., using Classification Web if your library has a subscription) or in the printed books. Write down the caption at the following numbers.

   a. QH540

   b. QH540.4

   c. QH540.8

   d. QH541

   e. QH541.15.A-Z

   f. QH541.15.E25

CHAPTER EIGHT
Locating Information

Introduction
An important skill for work, study and everyday life is being able to locate the information relevant to your needs quickly and efficiently.

If you need some information, where do you start looking? You might:
- ask a friend
- search the Internet
- look in books and other resources at home
- phone an advisory service
- visit a library or information service.

If you need to visit a library or information agency, how would you find out which are nearby? You could:
- look on the Internet
- check the telephone directory
    - Yellow Pages under Libraries, Information Services
    - White Pages under the name of the organization, association, government department or information agency
- ask friends and colleagues
- seek help at your local public library or Citizens' Advice Bureau.

How would you decide which library or information agency to use?
- What type of information do you need (e.g., specialized or general? indepth or at a basic level?)
- How quickly do you need the information?
- Can you pay to have the research done for you?

Factors to Consider When Choosing Which Information Agency to Use
- Subject strengths
    - does the information agency have materials relevant to your topic?
- Access and lending policy
    - is access restricted?
    - can you borrow or do you use the materials in the information agency?
    - are some materials not available for loan?
    - how many items can you borrow?
- Hours of opening
    - is the information agency open at times convenient to you? (Some information agencies are open in business hours only or offer limited services after hours)

- Scope of resources
  - are the resources at the right level for your needs?
  - does the information agency hold a range of formats?
  - does the information agency have access to databases?
- Range of services
  - is reference assistance available or is it 'self-help'?
  - does the information agency provide photocopying and computer facilities?
  - will the information agency obtain material from elsewhere if it is not held?
- Charges
  - is there a joining fee?
  - how much does photocopying cost?
  - are there charges for services such as online searching?

You might have to visit more than one information agency to find all the information you need.

Using a Library Efficiently

Libraries are one place where information can be sourced. Since libraries have been in existence for many years but information agencies are a new phenomenon, this section will concentrate on how to use a library, as an example of an information agency, efficiently.

Remember when using a library that information is available from a variety of sources. The Internet is just one source that you may search as it does not contain all available information. When using the Internet, check the reliability of the source. It is advisable to obtain information from a range of sources, both in print and electronic format. For that you need to search the library's catalog as a guide to its collection.

1. Check the library's catalog to find the location of the items you need and note down the call number and location symbol.

2. Look at the arrangement of the library's collection. Most libraries have materials shelved in several major sections:
   - main collection
   - reference collection
   - journal section
   - children's section
   - vertical file
   - audiovisual materials
   - short loan collections
   - audiovisual equipment section.

3. Determine which classification scheme the library uses. (DDC and LCC are the most common.)

4. Consult library guides or floor plans to find the relevant area of the collection.

5. If the item you need is not in the correct location on the shelf, you should check nearby shelves. If not there, re-check the call number and location symbol and make sure the item is not out on loan. You might need to look in a reshelving area or study area.

6. If this library does not hold the material you want, you may need to request an interlibrary loan, or consult a union catalog to find out which libraries hold the material.

7. Consult with a member of the library staff if you need further assistance.

Using a Library's Catalog
The catalog records all the items held in the library. As the catalog is the key to finding information in any library, learning how to use it is one of the most important skills in locating information.

Users look up the item according to what they know. For example, if they already know the title, they can find the item via the title, and then get the rest of the information they need (author, date of publication, call number and so on). If, however, they only know the subject, they look up the subject to find what the library has on it. A useful source of subject headings is the Library of Congress Subject Headings (the latest edition is accessible online at http://www.loc.gov/aba/cataloging/subject/).

80 LEARN ABOUT INFORMATION

EXERCISE 8.1

Look at the following examples of catalog entries and complete the exercise. The examples are taken from an OPAC of a large academic library.

1.

You searched for the AUTHOR: carver charles	
TITLE	Perspectives on personality / Charles S. Carver, Michael F. Scheier.
AUTHOR	Carver, Charles S.
OTHER AUTHOR	Scheier, Michael F.
EDITION	Seventh edition.
PUBLISHED	Boston : Pearson, 2012.
DESCRIPTION	xxvii, 450 pages : illustrations ; 27 cm.
SUBJECT	Personality
BIBLIOGRAPHY	Includes bibliographical references and indexes.
ISBN	9780205151363

	LOC'N	CALL #	STATUS
1	Central library	BF698.C22 2012	Available

a. What type of material is described in this catalog entry?

b. Who is the author?

c. Who published this item?

d. What is the date of publication?

e. Which edition is this publication?

f. Does the publication include an index?

g. Does the publication contain references?

h. What is this publication about?

i. How could you find other books on this subject?

j. Which classification scheme does this library use?

k. Where would you find this publication on the shelf?

l. How many copies would you expect to find on the shelf?

2.

You have searched for the keywords "DVD and Newton"	
CALL #	DVD 530.92 N563Ne
TITLE(S)	Newton's dark secrets [videorecording / a Blakeway Production for the BBC and WGBH Boston ; produced by Chris Oxley and Malcolm Neaum ; directed by Chris Oxley ; produced for NOVA by Joseph McMaster ; narration written by Joseph McMaster.
PUBLISHER	Boston : WGBH Boston Video, c2005.
DESCRIPTION	1 videodisc (56 min.) : sd., col. ; 4 3/4 in.
NOTES	Videodisc release of the documentary originally aired in 2005 on the PBS program, Nova. Special DVD-ROM features: teaching materials (PDF format) and a link to the Nova website. Editors, Nathan Hendrie, Safi Ferrah ; camera, Jon Wood, Rick Robertson, Joe Vitagliano ; music, Rob Morsberger, Robert Foster. Narrated by F. Murray Abraham. Isaac Newton portrayed by Scott Handy. DVD, all regions, letterbox presentation; Dolby Digital stereo. System requirements to access DVD-ROM features: Computer capable of reading PDF files, Internet access. Closed-captioned; described video.
SUMMARY	With vivid docudrama scenes, Nova recreates the climate of late 17th-century England, where a newfound fascination with science and mathematics coexisted with extreme views on religious doctrine. Unknown to most, Newton shared both obsessions, leading to experiments in alchemy along with his ground-breaking work in physics.
SUBJECT HEADINGS	Newton, Isaac, Sir, 1642-1727. Physicists Biography.
OTHER ENTRIES	Nova (Television program) Oxley, Christopher. Neaum, Malcolm. Abraham, F. Murray. McMaster, Joseph. Handy, Scott.
FORMAT	English Videodisc

a. What type of material is described in this catalog entry?

b. Who produced this resource?

c. Who is the publisher of this item?

d. What is this item about?

e. Does this item belong to a series?

f. What is the playing time of this item?

3.

You searched for the TITLE: contemporary sociology	
TITLE	Contemporary sociology.
AUTHOR	American Sociological Association.
PUBLISHED	[Albany, N.Y.] : American Sociological Association.
NOTE	Formerly issued as the Book review section of the American sociological review.
SUBJECT	Sociology - Book reviews - Periodicals.
ISSN	0094-3061.

1> Central Library serial HM1.C65
    LIB. HAS: 1:2(1972) - 22:2 (1993), 24:1(1995)-
    Latest received : November 2014 43:6
2> Departmental Library
    LIB. HAS: v.1 (1972) –

a. What type of material is described in this catalog entry?

b. When was the first issue of this publication published?

c. If you needed vol. 39, no. 3 of this publication, would this library have a copy?

d. What is the most recent issue received?

e. How would you find other items on this topic?

f. Has this publication changed its title?

EXERCISE 8.2

Using a library catalog available on the Internet, such as OCLC WorldCat (http://www.worldcat.org/) or the Library of Congress (http://catalog.loc.gov/) or the National Library of Australia's Trove (http://trove.nla.gov.au/), find the answers to the following questions. Write down your answers and the search you conducted to find them.

1. What is the title of the book written by Simon W. Bowmaker about the practice of economics research in 2012?

2. I have heard of a book titled *Fundamentals of software testing* which was published in Hoboken, New Jersey in 2012 and I need to know who the author is?

3. What is the name of the publisher of *Total stock car racing*?

4. Does the book *Principles of yacht design* which was published by International Marine/McGraw-Hill Education contain any illustrations? Who are the authors?

5. Who publishes the electronic journal *Geology*?

6. Is there a list of music on the sound recording *Treasure chest* by Decca produced in about 1957?

7. Has the *Histochemical journal* changed its title?

8. What is the edition number of *Clinical neuroanatomy* written by Stephen Waxman and published in 2013?

9. What is the ISBN for the book about Van Gogh written by Steven Naifeh and Gregory White Smith that was published in 2011 by Random House?

10. When did the periodical *Criminal behaviour and mental health* begin publication?

The Reference Collection
The reference collection or section in a library contains resources that users refer to for particular pieces of information. For example, people may refer to a dictionary for the spelling of a word, or an atlas to find a place.

These resources have traditionally been in printed form, but many are also available online. Sometimes it is easier to look up information in a book, and at other times on a computer. Most libraries have both types of reference resources, and different users will choose one form or the other at different times.

When you begin to find information on a subject, the first step is to define exactly what you want to know. It is often useful to start with a reference resource, since dictionaries and encyclopedias, in particular, provide brief introductory explanations of subjects, and are usually easy to use.

The reference section consists of dictionaries, encyclopedias, directories, yearbooks, handbooks, manuals, geographical sources and bibliographies. These resources provide quick concise answers to questions and are usually not available for loan.

Dictionaries
Dictionaries are used to find the meaning of words, their origin, their pronunciation and grammatical context. There are many categories of dictionary (e.g., foreign language, children's, historical, regional, crossword, slang, synonyms and antonyms, abbreviations and acronyms and subject dictionaries). Examples include the *Concise Oxford dictionary*; *Roget's thesaurus*; *Acronyms, initialisms and abbreviations dictionary*.

Encyclopedias
Encyclopedias are used to find a summary on a subject or to find background information and recommended reading. There are many types of encyclopedia (e.g., general, subject, national and foreign language). Examples include *Encyclopaedia Britannica*; the *Oxford encyclopedia of British literature*; *World book encyclopedia*; and the *Audubon Society encyclopedia of North American birds*.

Directories
Directories are a useful starting point when you want to find information about people and organizations. They usually provide names, addresses, telephone numbers and brief details about organizations or associations. Categories include local, government, institutional and professional, trade and business directories. Old directories are often useful for historical research. Examples include *International who's who* and *Chamber's biographical dictionary* (about people) and *International sports medicine directory*; *Directory of Australian associations* and *World of learning* (for organizations).

Yearbooks, Handbooks and Manuals
These contain miscellaneous facts and statistics on a variety of topics. They are revised frequently to ensure the information is up-to-date. Examples include *Europa world year book*, *Whitaker's almanack* and *The classic outboard motor handbook*. These publications are usually treated as serials.

Geographical Sources
These provide information about places and geographical features. The most common geographical sources are maps, atlases and gazetteers. Examples include the *Times atlas of the world* and the *Columbia Lippincott gazetteer of the world*.

EXERCISE 8.3

Match each of the following types of reference books with the correct description below.

Dictionary	A list of related library materials or resources, usually subject related
Encyclopedia	An alphabetically arranged publication containing information about words, meanings, derivations, spelling, pronunciation, syllabication and usage
Index	A systematic summary of all significant knowledge; a summary of the knowledge of one subject. Usually arranged alphabetically
Yearbook	An annual publication containing current information in brief, descriptive and/or statistical form
Handbook	A list of names of residents, organizations or firms in a city, region, country or internationally, providing various details (e.g., addresses; a list of members in a particular profession or trade)
Almanac	A book written primarily for practitioners and serving as a book for constant revision or reference
Bibliography	A book of instruction on doing, making or performing something
Directory	A systematically arranged list which indicates the contents of a document or group of documents
Atlas	An annual calendar with astronomical information and other data: a miscellany of useful facts and statistical information
Gazetteer	A volume of maps either to show locations or on a particular theme
Biographical directory	A listing of people, usually in alphabetical order of surname, providing details of dates, titles, birthplace, family, etc.
Manual	A geographical directory listing places, and their locations

88 LEARN ABOUT INFORMATION

EXERCISE 8.4

Find answers to the following questions using printed reference sources. Write down the answers and the reference source where you found them.

1. What is the meaning of the word gecko?

2. Can you find a synonym for the word habitual?

3. Where can I find some illustrations of flags of the world?

4. Could you find some information on the life of Florence Nightingale?

5. When was Pierre Elliott Trudeau the Prime Minister of Canada?

6. What does the acronym GOTA stand for?

7. What is a palindrome?

8. Who was John Braine?

9. Where would you find information about the experiences of African Americans in the United States?

10. What does smidgen mean?

11. What are John Kerry's hobbies?

12. What is the address of the Australian Tourist Commission in Los Angeles?

13. When was the University of Oxford founded?

14. Where would I find some information about religion in Denmark?

15. What was the median household income in Luxembourg in 2011?

16. When did the singer Placido Domingo make his operatic debut?

17. When was David Cameron first elected to the British Parliament?

18. When did Rudyard Kipling die?

19. When did the tennis player, Serena Williams last win the Wimbledon title?

20. What is the main objective of UNESCO?

Bibliographies

Bibliographies provide citations rather than full-text listings to help you find sources on a particular topic or by a particular author. You can obtain a unique description of each item and check details for accuracy. In libraries, this bibliographic verification is important for a variety of processes such as acquisitions, interlibrary loans or reference work as well as in preparing bibliographies for users.

Types of Bibliographies
- National bibliographies:
    - provide a systematic list of publications published in one country or in one language
    - include items received under legal deposit and cataloged by a national agency
    - are usually arranged in classified order with detailed indexes.

    Until recently, many countries produced printed national bibliographies; however these have been replaced by electronic versions. Examples include:
    - *Canadiana* (http://amicus.collectionscanada.ca/aaweb/aalogine.htm)
    - *Deutsche Nationalbibliographie* (http://www.dnb.de/EN/nationalbibliografie)
    - *British national bibliography* (http://bnb.bl.uk/)
    - *Australian national bibliographic database*, that is available by subscription at (http://www.nla.gov.au/librariesaustralia/) or available free to the public through Trove (http://trove.nla.gov.au/).

- Trade bibliographies are produced from information supplied by publishers and include items for sale and in print. Their information may not conform to library description standards. They include publications irrespective of the date that they were published. As with other bibliographic tools, printed trade bibliographies have been replaced by electronic versions. Examples of trade bibliographies include *Books in print* (http://www.booksinprint.com/), and *Ulrichsweb global serials directory* (http://ulrichsweb.serialssolutions.com/).

    The websites of individual publishers and booksellers also provide bibliographic details of available publications.

- Subject bibliographies list material on a particular topic such as *International bibliography of sign language.*

EXERCISE 8.5

Examine the websites of the following bibliographic sources and find the following information for each title.
  a. *Type of bibliographic tool (e.g., national, trade)*
  b. *Publisher*
  c. *Frequency*
  d. *Subject coverage*
  e. *Format coverage*
  f. *Access points (how you search the database)*
  g. *Arrangement (e.g., classified, alphabetical)*

Books in print (http://www.booksinprint.com/)

British national bibliography (http://bnb.bl.uk/)

Canadiana (http://amicus.collectionscanada.ca/aaweb/aalogine.htm)

Ulrichsweb global serials directory (http://www.ulrichsweb.com/ulrichsweb/faqs.asp)

Which Bibliographic Tool to Use?
1. Decide what information you have and what information you are looking for (e.g., you have author and title but need publication details).
2. Do you want a monograph, a serial or an article?
3. Can you determine the country of origin? Some bibliographic tools have materials from only one country.
4. Do you know the date of publication? Some bibliographic tools are easier to use if you have some idea of the date.
5. Do you want a commercial publication? If not, trade bibliographies will not help.

EXERCISE 8.6

Decide which library source you would use to answer each of the following questions. Match each question to a different source.

Question	Library Source
In what year did President John F. Kennedy die?	Library catalog / union catalog
How old was Peter Jennings when he died?	Internet
Does my library hold any books about Emily Dickinson? If my library doesn't, which libraries do?	Subject bibliography
Where can I find a bibliography of poems from the First World War?	Trade bibliography
Are any works by Henry David Thoreau still in print?	Biographical dictionary

CHAPTER NINE
Presenting Information

Introduction
The previous chapters have described how to locate and organize information. The next important step is to present this information in a manner appropriate to the user or audience.

Presenting Information - How Will You Convey the Information?
When you have gathered and organized your information, you need to decide how to present it. Sometimes this will be decided for you. For example, you may be asked for a written report, an oral presentation or a bibliography.

There are many ways in which information can be presented. The style of presentation will depend on the audience and on the type of information being presented.

Formats for Presenting Information Include

- bibliographies
- blogs
- computer programs
- debates
- demonstrations
- drama
- electronic reports
- films
- instruction programs
- lectures
- mock trials
- models
- pamphlets
- pictures
- poems
- posters
- powerpoints
- radio
- reading lists
- role plays
- seminars
- social media
- TV
- verbal reports
- workbooks
- written reports

Each form of presentation has different requirements. If you are presenting a verbal report, you may include charts, graphs or a video to illustrate a point. You might need to arrange special equipment before presenting your report.

Effective Presentations Involve:
- planning the presentation (determining the task, purpose and audience)
- deciding on format and sequence
- selecting and/or developing instructional materials (e.g., PowerPoint presentation, handouts)
- dealing with anxiety and nerves
- establishing a rapport with the group.

Writing a Report

One of the most common ways of presenting information is a written report. Most people, either in the workplace or as part of their studies, will be required to prepare a report. Mastering report writing is an essential skill in many professions, whether it is a simple work procedure or a more official technical analysis.

What is a Report?

A report is a written statement of a situation, project, process or test which includes:
- the facts
- how the facts were obtained
- their significance
- conclusions
- recommendations.

Reports vary in length, appearance, purpose and formality, but they all present accurate factual information as a basis for informed evaluation. The purpose or major aim of the report will determine what type of report is written.

All reports should present information and ideas in an organized, clear, accurate, interesting and readable way. A report follows a standard format and uses headings and subheadings to help the reader find information quickly.

Uses of Reports

Reports have several purposes. The main uses are to:
- record work done
- present data to keep people informed
- assess a situation
- validate information
- provide a basis for decision-making
- present recommendations
- save duplication of effort
- circulate new ideas
- indicate future action
- evaluate a program.

Preparing a Report

Reports are produced in six stages:
- clarification of instructions
  - make sure you understand what is required
- careful preparation
  - collect relevant information and watch out for irrelevant facts
- organize the information
  - arrange information in sections under headings
- plan and organize the layout
  - organize a logical progression of headings and sections
- writing

- be objective
- write in a clear, concise manner using logical sentence construction
- don't cram too much onto one page
- review
  - correct factual, spelling and grammatical errors
  - check that all the essential information is included and that it is accurate and verifiable
  - make sure the report is not too long.

Structure of the Report
Reports generally follow a standard layout and format. The sections are:
- Executive Summary
- Introduction
- Body
- Conclusions
- Recommendations
- Bibliography
- Appendices.

Executive Summary
An executive summary is a short document that summarizes the full report. It allows the reader to quickly grasp the concepts contained in the report without having to read it all. The executive summary usually contains a brief statement of the issue covered in the report, background information, concise analysis and main conclusions. (Not all reports require an executive summary but they are frequently used in business reports.)

Introduction
The introduction states the purpose of the report, outlines the scope of the topic covered or any limitations, and describes how the information was obtained.

For example, if you are writing a report on two information agencies, you should name the agencies, say why you chose them, comment on any limitations (e.g., you might decide to describe one section of the National Library of Medicine rather than the library as a whole), and finally describe how you obtained your information.

Body
This is the main information section, which presents the facts and incorporates the major points in a logical manner. It can be divided into sections such as Findings and Discussion with each section subdivided. Headings enable the reader to locate information quickly. In the discussion, the writer interprets the evidence presented in the findings and links the evidence with the aim or purpose of the report.

Conclusion
The conclusion is the writer's interpretation of the evidence.

Recommendations
This section proposes specific action to be taken based on the conclusions.

Bibliography
The bibliography is a list of the sources consulted. The list is usually arranged in alphabetical order and follows a standard format. Before preparing your bibliography, decide (or check with your supervisor) which style to use. The bibliography enables the reader to consult the writer's reference material.

Appendices
The appendix or appendices provide supporting or additional material (e.g., tables, charts, diagrams).

Presentation
The appearance of the report should be an invitation to the reader. Care should be taken with paragraphing, headings and space so that the report looks clear and legible. An inviting cover would be an advantage. A contents page is also valuable. Ensure that you spell-check and proofread before presenting the report.

Preparing a Bibliography
Working in an information agency often involves compiling bibliographies for clients to assist them in their research requests.

A bibliography can be defined in a number of ways, but this workbook reflects the following definitions:

> "A list of books of a particular author, printer, country, etc.; a list of works consulted in a scholarly work; a reading list." (*The new shorter Oxford English dictionary*)

> "A list of materials or resources, usually either subject-related or on the works of one author" (*LibrarySpeak*)

When arranging this information, it is important that each citation contains details in the same order. This way the user can easily see the author, title, date of publication and so on. Bibliographies are usually arranged alphabetically, primarily by author.

Bibliographical Styles
There are a number of bibliographical styles that can be used to present a bibliography. Whichever style you choose, it is important to maintain consistency. The more common styles used include: Harvard (that is also referred to as the Author – date system) referencing style (http://www.hup.harvard.edu/resources/authors/pdf/hup-author-guidelines-author-date-citations-and-reference-lists.pdf), the MLA (Modern Language Association) referencing system (http://www.mla.org/style); and the APA (American Psychological Association) style (http://www.apastyle.org/). Another useful tool that provides recommendations on styles is *The Chicago manual of style* (http://www.chicagomanualofstyle.org/home.html).

No matter which bibliographical style you use, the following points should be included in the citations that are prepared.

- List references in alphabetical order by the first author's or editor's name, with surname first.
- If the author is unknown, list using the title instead, ignoring the initial words 'the', 'a' and 'an'.
- Italicize or underline the title of the resource.
- If no place of publication is given, use [Place of publication not identified] and if no date, use [date of publication not identified].
- Include playing time for films and DVDs.

Different formats of material require different information to be included in the bibliography. The following bibliographic elements should be included to help users identify items in a bibliography.

Electronic sources
- author(s), editor(s), compiler(s) or the institution/organization responsible for the resource
- title and subtitle
- edition
- type of medium (e.g., online, CD-ROM)
- information supplier if appropriate
- full address (including path if applicable) to find the resource
- date of access.

Books (monographs)
- author(s), editor(s), compiler(s) or the institution/organization responsible for the resource
- title and subtitle
- edition
- place and date of publication
- publisher
- series.

Journal (serial) articles
- author(s) of article
- title of article
- title of journal
- issue details
- page numbers.

Non-book items
- author(s), editor(s), compiler(s) or the institution/organization responsible for the resource
- title and subtitle
- edition

- type of medium (e.g., DVD, map)
- series
- publisher
- place of publication.

 Here is a short bibliography developed from the information given below. Note the arrangement of the citations into alphabetical order by their first element (author or title).

author:	Yushiou Tsai, Sara Cohen and Richard M. Vogel
title:	The impacts of water conservation strategies on water use: four case studies
journal:	Journal of the American Water Resources Association
volume:	47, issue 4
date:	August 2011
pages:	687-701
URL:	http://onlinelibrary.wiley.com/doi/10.1111/j.1752-1688.2011.00534.x/pdf
accessed:	November 27, 2014

author:	Sonia Ferdous Hoque
title:	Water conservation in urban households
subtitle:	role of prices, policies and technologies
place:	London
publisher:	IWA Publishing
date:	2014

title:	Earth aid water conservation
producer:	Mike Bloom, Rick Larsen
place:	New York
publisher:	V.I.E.W. Inc.
date:	2006
format:	DVD
playing time:	20 minutes

Suggested arrangement:

Earth aid water conservation. Produced by Mike Bloom and Rick Larsen. New York, V.I.E.W. Inc., 2006. DVD, 20 min.

Hoque, Sonia Ferdous. *Water conservation In urban households: role of prices, policies and technologies.* London, IWA Publishing, 2014.

Tsai, Yushiou, Sara Cohen, and Richard M. Vogel. 'The impacts of water conservation strategies on water use: four case studies'. *Journal of the American Water Resources Association* 47, no. 4 (2011): 687-701. http://onlinelibrary.wiley.com/doi/10.1111/j.1752-1688.2011.00534.x/pdf

EXERCISE 9.1

Choose a bibliographic style to present the bibliography below. Consider using Harvard, MLA, APA, or Chicago.

Arrange the following correctly in the bibliographic style you have chosen:

author:	Nancy J. Ondra
title:	Five plant garden
subtitle:	52 ways to grow a perennial garden with just five plants
place:	North Adams, MA
publisher:	Storey Publishing
date:	2014

author:	Gail Ann Langellotto
title:	What are the economic costs and benefits of home vegetable gardens?
journal:	Journal of Extension
volume:	Volume 52, number 2
date:	April 2014
pages:	2-5
URL:	http://www.joe.org/joe/2014april/rb5.php
accessed:	November 27, 2014

author:	Kenneth Cox and Ray Cox
title:	Scotland for gardeners
subtitle:	the ultimate guide to Scottish gardens, nurseries and garden centres
edition	New
place:	Edinburgh
publisher:	Birlinn
date:	2014

author:	Phipps Conservatory and Botanical Gardens
title:	Your guide to Phipps Conservatory and Botanical Gardens
place:	Pittsburgh
publisher:	Phipps Conservatory and Botanical Gardens
date:	2014
format:	1 map

author:	Stephanie Alexander
title:	Stephanie Alexander Kitchen Garden Foundation
place:	Melbourne
publisher:	Stephanie Alexander Kitchen Garden Foundation
date:	Last modified November 7 2014
URL:	http://www.kitchengardenfoundation.org.au/

author:	Katherine Alaimo, Elizabeth Packnett, Richard A. Miles, Daniel J. Kruger
title:	Fruit and vegetable intake among urban community gardeners
journal:	Journal of Nutrition Education and Behavior
volume:	Volume 40, Issue 2
date:	March–April 2008
pages:	94-101
URL:	doi:10.1016/j.jneb.2006.12.003
accessed:	November 27, 2014

director:	Makoto Shinkai.
title:	The garden of words
place:	Richmond, Victoria
publisher:	Sentai filmworks
date:	2014
format:	DVD
playing time:	116 min.

author:	Rachael L. Jaenke, Clare E. Collins, Philip J. Morgan, David R. Lubans, Kristen L. Saunders and Janet M. Warren
title:	The impact of a school garden and cooking program on boys' and girls' fruit and vegetable preferences, taste rating, and intake
journal:	Health Education & Behavior
volume:	39
date:	April 2012
pages:	131-141
URL:	http://heb.sagepub.com/content/39/2/131.full.pdf+html
accessed:	November 27, 2014

author:	Kim Flottum
title:	The backyard beekeeper
subtitle:	an absolute beginner's guide to keeping bees in your yard and garden
edition:	3rd
place:	Beverley, MA
publisher:	Quarry Books
date:	2014
series:	Backyard series

author:	Percy Grainger
title:	Country gardens
place:	[Wokingham, UK]
publisher:	Julian Dyer
date:	201-?
format:	1 piano roll

author: Katherine Rinne
title: Garden hydraulics in pre-sistine Rome: theory and practice
chapter: 6
In: author: Michael G. Lee and Kenneth I. Helphand (eds)
title: Technology and the garden
place: Washington, DC
publisher: Dumbarton Oaks
date: 2014
series: Dumbarton Oaks colloquium on the history of landscape architecture; no. 35

author: Jacob Biggle
title: Biggle orchard book
subtitle: fruit and orchard gleanings from bough to basket
place: Philadelphia
volume: Skyhorse Publishing
date: 2014
format: Ebook

Citation Tools

Bibliographies can be arranged using citation management tools that are a useful way to collect and cite the sources you use. Citation tools are online resources that allow you to record bibliographic details when they are accessed rather than waiting till the complete list is ready to be compiled. Five of the most popular citation management tools are *Zotero, Calibre, Mendeley, EndNote,* and *RefWorks*.

Some citation tools can be used without charge, for example:
- *Zotero* (http://www.zotero.org/) is a citation manager designed to store, manage, and cite bibliographic references, including books, PDFs, images, audio and video files, and snapshots of web pages.
- *Calibre* (http://calibre-ebook.com/) is a free and open source e-book computer software application that organizes, saves, and manages e-books. *Calibre* is available for Windows, OSX, and Linux and can be synchronized with a variety of popular e-book readers. It can also convert online content sources, including news articles, into e-books.

Other citation tools have a basic version that is available free but have the option for a paid version with more features:
- *Mendeley* (http://www.mendeley.com/) is a desktop and web program for managing and sharing research papers, discovering research data, and collaborating online. It combines *Mendeley Desktop*, a PDF and reference management application (available for Windows, OSX and Linux) with *Mendeley Web*, an online social network for researchers.
- *EndNote* (http://endnote.com/) is a reference management software package used to manage bibliographies and references. With it you can group citations into 'libraries'. It can also be integrated with Microsoft Word.

Some citation tools have been set up as commercial software packages. They are often free to students and staff of a university or organization to use, but are otherwise a paid service.
- *RefWorks* (http://www.refworks.com/) is a citation management software program that collects, stores, and organizes citations from books, articles, websites, and other sources. It is a web-based service that can be used with any of the major web browsers on any platform.

Oral Presentations

Students often need to prepare a small group presentation or talk, in order to equip them with the skills for making verbal reports in the workplace. These may be informal talks or more formal speeches.

The following guidelines should assist in the presentation of a talk, but, as with most tasks, skill will come with careful preparation and with practice at performing the task.

Purpose
When planning a talk, you must be clear about the purpose of the presentation. Most small group presentations aim to *inform, persuade* and/or *amuse*. Presentations usually report the results of individual research or demonstrate knowledge.

Preparation
Research your topic thoroughly. Confidence comes from knowing your topic. Even if you do not use all your gathered information in the talk, the extra knowledge may come in handy when answering questions or referring your audience to more information.

When planning your presentation, a few relevant facts may be of more use to your audience than strings of dates or lists of data. This sort of information may be useful as a handout.

Organizing the Talk
Like a good report, a presentation requires careful organization. Most speeches are organized in three parts: (1) the introduction, (2) the body, and (3) the conclusion.

Introduction
This is where you need to gain the attention of the audience as you outline the intention and scope of your presentation. You may wish to indicate the basic structure of the talk.

There are a number of delivery devices that can be used other than the boring 'This talk is about...' opening sentence. You could:
- make a startling statement or state an interesting fact
- ask a rhetorical question
- quote a recognized authority
- refer to an occasion
- state your opinion.

These devices, if used, must be relevant to the topic. An irrelevant joke or statement will confuse the audience and distract their attention from the content of the talk.

Whichever introduction technique you use, the introduction must
- indicate the topic
- explain the scope of the talk
- gain audience attention.

Content
In a short talk, only two or three main points can be developed fully to the satisfaction of the audience. All points should relate to the theme described in the introduction. The body of your presentation should be structured in order of importance, in chronological order, or in logical order.

Conclusion
Have a well prepared concluding statement that summarizes the theme and challenges the audience to think further about the subject. The conclusion should be linked to the introduction and not be used to introduce new topics.

Delivery

Never read a presentation, as it implies that you are unfamiliar with the topic, and lack confidence. It is often a good idea to summarize your talk into point form, then write it on a single piece of paper, or on cards. Refer to the sheet or cards throughout the talk. Use them as an aid to remembering the next point. Practice your presentation but do not memorize it completely as you can easily forget a point, or lose track of the theme.

A talk should have both visual and vocal impact.

Visual Impact
- Establish brief eye contact with your audience as this involves them with the talk.
- Appear relaxed and comfortable, preferably standing in front of the audience.
- Do not move excessively as this is distracting.
- Be aware of nervous gestures.
- Smile, be confident and enthusiastic. This is easy if you know your subject.

Vocal Impact
- Use clear, distinct speech.
- Talk at a normal pace, not too fast or too slow.
- Vary the pitch and volume of your voice naturally.
- Use pauses to emphasize points or a change in topic.
- Do not use jargon without explaining the terms.
- Never say 'um'.

Visual Aids

Visual aids help the audience to
- follow your talk
- visually understand points
- look at something other than the speaker
- write notes on the topic.

These aids could include:
- PowerPoint presentation
- slides and video tapes
- handout material
- physical examples of material
- charts, posters, maps
- graphs
- whiteboard.

Ensure that all visual aids are relevant and add to your presentation. Ensure they can be seen, are legibly produced, and are not cluttered in appearance. Make sure the correct equipment is available to view them.

Display your visual aids at the correct time in your talk and remove them after referring to them.

Remember that the visual aids need to be relevant to your talk, and are not to be used to distract the audience from the content of the talk.

Stage Fright?
Prepare, practice and try to remember that your audience usually wants you to succeed. Prepare a planning sheet to help you take control of the situation. The planning sheet should detail each step, what resources you will need, and an estimate of the time you will spend on each point.

You should also:
- take a deep breath
- enjoy and know your topic
- recognize that your stressful feelings are common to most people
- stand tall and smile at the audience. Remember they are only people.

Evaluating—What Did You Learn From This?
The final stage is to decide whether you have fulfilled your purpose. You need to discover whether your presentation met the audience's or client's expectations. You also need to consider how you would improve your performance if you had to do a similar task again.

You could undertake an evaluation exercise by asking your audience to provide you with feedback. This could be as an informal discussion or in the form of an evaluation sheet. You should tell you audience that they are not judging you, but providing helpful feedback which will enable you to improve your presentations.

A self-evaluation is also helpful, where you assess whether you have achieved your original purpose, what aspects of your presentation were successful, what aspects could be improved and how you personally felt about your experience.

Future successful presentations could depend upon your willingness to adapt or modify a presentation, either in delivery style or in content.

EXERCISE 9.2

Research a topic of your choice. For instance, you may like to choose a famous person and include information such as: where and when the person was born; why the person is famous; what has been written about them.

Write a half page report on the topic, using the following method:
- *define the problem and outline a search strategy*
- *use as many sources of information as you can to locate relevant information*
- *record the details of the sources used*
- *decide which was the most useful source and give reasons for your choice*
- *summarize the information collected.*

If possible, present the information before your fellow students or colleagues, using a suitable format.
Either together with others, or on your own, evaluate your research, your report and your presentation.

CHAPTER TEN
Libraries as Information Agencies

Introduction
Information is a commodity that is shared and made available by all sorts of organizations. Libraries are the most established and well-known of the information agencies. Therefore, this chapter focuses on libraries as examples of information agencies.

What Are Libraries?
Libraries are organized collections of documents, films, maps, sound recordings and other forms of media, that are designed to meet the informational, educational and recreational needs of a given user population. These types of collections may also be housed in media centers, educational resource centers, and information, documentation and referral centers.

Although many information agencies have devised their own individual methods for organizing and arranging their collections, libraries have developed standards for the way collections are described and classified. Standardization, in areas such as library catalogs, classification schemes, and subject analysis, is one of the defining characteristic of libraries that sets them apart from other information agencies. Users everywhere around the world are able to have a similar experience when visiting a library and can access library collections because of the standardized methodologies that are used.

Basic Aims of Libraries
Libraries aim to satisfy users' information needs by obtaining, organizing, providing and preserving print and non-print materials, and access to electronic resources.

Methods used by libraries to fulfil these aims depend on:
- the type of library
- client needs
- types of material held
- organizational constraints such as:
    - staff
    - finance
    - space
    - other resources.

Similarly, other organizations produce and provide information. Libraries often use these agencies to gather information, or refer users to their collections.

Types of Libraries
The main types of libraries that serve the differing information needs of the community are:
- national libraries
- state libraries
- public libraries
- academic libraries
- special libraries
- school libraries.

Organizational Structure of Libraries
Not all libraries are set up with the same organizational model. However, the organizational structure usually remains the same regardless of the type of library, the number of staff and the range of users. The three divisions in the traditional structure of a library are administration, public services (also known as reader services or client services) and technical services. These three divisions may overlap in smaller libraries.

Administration
Administrative duties include:
- management
- policy decisions
- budget control
- staff supervision
- personnel matters
- staff training
- liaison within the organization
- liaison with other organizations
- providing advice
- planning
- information technology (IT) support.

Many of these duties are performed by professional librarians, professional managers and other allied personnel.

Public Services
The public services section (also known as client services or reader services) provides for library users through the registration of clients, instruction in library use, meeting users' requests for specific information and assistance and managing the use and loan of library material and equipment.

This area is the main point of contact with clients. Specific services in this area include:
- loans
- reader education
- user assistance

Loans
A loan is a recorded transaction in which a borrower removes an item from a collection for a stated period. A record should be created when an item is borrowed. This record contains bibliographic details of the item borrowed (e.g., author, title, barcode), details of the borrower and due date.

Other tasks at the loans desk may include returns, reserves, recalls, renewals, overdue items and fines.

Some libraries (e.g., national and state libraries) do not lend items (except on interlibrary loan) so all items must be viewed within the library. Other libraries may restrict borrowing to certain types of material or restrict the loan period for material in high demand. Generally, reference resources or periodicals are not circulated.

Interlibrary Loan (ILL)
Interlibrary loan or document delivery is a loan by one library to another for the use of an individual, or the provision of a photocopy or digital copy of the resource requested. The purpose of interlibrary loan is to obtain access to more material, to avoid duplication and to save money. Interlibrary lending can be done electronically via a library network, by email, by fax, or by phone. Although it can be costly in time, resources and staff, it does allow clients access to a wider range of materials.

Borrowing between libraries may be free, especially between libraries with similar clients and collections (for example health libraries), or in a certain locality.

Interlibrary Loan Code
A number of countries (including Australia with the *Australian interlibrary resource sharing (ILRS)* code, and the United States with the *Interlibrary code for the United States*) have established codes to facilitate efficient and equitable sharing of resources held in libraries in their countries. Participating libraries agree to:
- not overburden the system—a library may need to review its selection policy if it is constantly requesting material
- comply with written and unwritten rules
- verify details before requesting an item (i.e., provide the correct title, author, serial issue, etc.)
- observe copyright requirements by completing declaration forms when requesting photocopying
- adhere to restrictions on use (e.g., the item must be used in the library when asked)
- not request valuable or rare materials, reference items or complete journal volumes
- use proper safe delivery (e.g., courier, certified mail)
- return material on time and in its original condition.

Reader Education
Users are instructed on how to use the resources of a library (e.g., the catalog, reference materials, databases and the Internet). This may involve demonstrations, audiovisual

presentations, lectures, tours, booklists or leaflets, and can be given to individuals or to groups.

Different libraries use different methods to educate their users:
- school libraries schedule timetabled classes
- academic libraries arrange tours in orientation week or conduct tutorials
- academic libraries also provide tutorials on websites
- special libraries often teach one-to-one as needed
- public libraries give assistance individually, or in printed guides.

Reference Services

Library staff provide their users with assistance in using the library's collection and services. They also offer expertise on information from a diverse range of sources. Specific reference services include:
- ready reference enquiries: These are short, directional or factual answers (for example, 'Who is our local Congressman or Member of Parliament?', 'Where are the books on dogs?')
- research enquiries: Libraries sometimes charge for these services which may involve:
    - compiling bibliographies
    - assembling reading lists on special topics
    - answering detailed subject enquiries
    - verifying data and bibliographic information
    - performing electronic searches of databases, and/or the Internet
- current awareness services: These are provided to keep users up-to-date with information in their interest or subject areas, and are often delivered directly to the user's desktop. Specific services include:
    - bibliographies
    - journal circulation
    - displays
    - new items lists
    - circulation of title and/or contents pages
    - indexes and abstracts
    - newspaper clippings
    - bookmarking relevant Internet sites
    - current awareness bulletins
    - RSS feeds.

Readers' Advisory

This service is mainly provided in public libraries. Library staff (known as readers' advisors) help users to find recreational reading that interests them. This requires knowledge of the collection, especially the fiction collection, and an appreciation of the range of fiction genres available. Books on animals, arts and entertainment, biography and memoir, discovery, food, gardening, history, home improvement, humor, travel, and true crime are also of interest to recreational readers.

Services to Distinct User Groups
Special services are provided for particular groups of users. Special user groups include:
- children (reading groups, holiday programs, book week, toy libraries)
- people with disabilities (braille, large print and talking books, captioned DVDs)
- the aged (home services, clubs)
- the housebound (mobile library and home services)
- users of non English-speaking background (other community language material)
- people with literacy concerns (literacy programs)
- residents of outlying districts (mobile library services).

Publicity and Public Relations
This includes marketing the library services to potential clients in a variety of ways (for example special displays, events, courses, newspaper articles, newsletters).

Technical Services
This section of a library acquires and organizes resources for users. Items flow through sections of technical services, and eventually enter the public area of the library, or are accessed online via computer terminals located in the library and offsite. Specific technical services activities include:
- Acquisitions
- Cataloging
- Final Processing.

Acquisitions
Acquisitions staff obtain new material for the library's collection. Their tasks include ordering, receiving, and recording receipt of all new library material.

Cataloging
This section maintains bibliographic control of the library's collection. The staff produce records that describe items, assign classification numbers and subject headings, and record these details in the catalog.

Final Processing
After items have been cataloged, they are prepared for loan and/or use in the library. This commonly involves labeling and adding security tape to the material. Non-book material is packaged so that it can be shelved and borrowed easily.

Library Staffing
Traditionally, library staff are described by dividing them into four categories:
- professional
- paraprofessional
- clerical
- support.

Professional

The librarian or teacher-librarian has library qualifications (usually a three-year Bachelors degree, a Masters degree or a Graduate Diploma), is recognized as a professional by the relevant library association and/or performs work at a professional level. Teacher-librarians usually have teaching and library qualifications.

A professional selects, organizes, manages and disseminates material, often in a managerial or supervisory role, and is concerned with the *development* and *overall management* of the library.

Paraprofessional

The library technician/officer/assistant has a qualification (usually a two-year diploma) recognized as paraprofessional by the relevant library association, or performs work at a paraprofessional level.

A paraprofessional supports the library's professional staff and is involved with the operation, maintenance and control of established systems (i.e., in an *operational* role).

Clerical

People in this position are usually *directed* to tasks by the professionals or paraprofessionals supervising them. They are often trained on the job and would need some library training to perform higher-level duties.

Support

Large libraries often employ non-library-trained staff to work in *support* of the administrative section. These staff include experts in information technology, administrative staff in personnel sections, and security, cleaning and maintenance staff.

Staff duties depend on:
- the type of library
- the size of library
- the number of staff
- the personality of staff
- changing work flows
- whether work rotation is encouraged.

Exercise 10.1

Answer the following questions about the library in which you work, or study, or another library with which you are familiar.

1. What hours is the library open?

2. Where is the loans desk and why is it located there?

3. Is any material available explaining how to use the library?

4. How many items can you borrow from the library?

5. How do you borrow a book? What are the advantages of this system? Can you suggest any disadvantages or improvements?

6. Name 5 types of material held in the library.

7. Where are the reference materials shelved and why are they shelved there?

8. Is the reference/enquiry desk staffed all the time?

9. Locate a reference book on the shelves. How does it indicate that it is reference?

10. Where are the DVDs shelved?

11. List what formats of resources are available for clients to use in the library. Which of these can be borrowed?

12. How would you find out if a periodical is held in the library? Where are the recent issues of periodicals shelved? Are periodicals in print, electronic format or both?

13. Describe the notices and signs that help readers use the library more effectively.

14. List all the sources you would use in the library to find information on a topic.

15. Can you find a map of the library and/or its location in the city or on campus?

16. Does the library provide electronic databases to its clients? If yes, list two of these.

17. Where are the fiction titles shelved in the library?

18. How would you reserve an item that is out on loan?

19. Can clients access the Internet in the library? Can clients access the library off site?

20. Does the library cater for different client groups?

CHAPTER ELEVEN
Different Library Environments

Introduction
In Chapter 10 we examined the roles that libraries play in the information environment. This chapter considers the main types of libraries that serve the differing information needs of the community:
- National libraries
- State libraries
- Public libraries
- Joint-use libraries
- Academic libraries
- School libraries
- Special libraries.

National Libraries
A national library is a library that has been established by the government of a country to serve as the primary repository of information for that country. Some national libraries have been created by dividing the national collections, as was the case with the British Library that split from the British Museum in 1973. In Canada, the reverse situation occurred, as the national library and archives collections merged in 2004 to form the new Libraries and Archives Canada. Some national libraries, such as the National Library of Australia, have been formed by legislation. The United States has established a number of national libraries, divided by subject—Library of Congress, National Library of Medicine, National Agricultural Library, National Library of Education, and the National Transportation Library—where each plays its role as a national collection, but the Library of Congress is the de facto national library of the United States.

A national library is maintained out of government funds and serves the nation as a whole. It is usually the country's legal deposit library, and collects and preserves the nation's literature. Legal deposit is a legal requirement that copies of publications are submitted to a repository, usually a library.

National libraries:
- are major providers of information services
- are the central agencies for creating and disseminating bibliographic data and other support services
- coordinate national library networks, providing and supporting a wide range of resource sharing and other cooperative services
- are national heritage institutions, acquiring and preserving a comprehensive collection of unique culturally significant works.

Their clients include other libraries, researchers, archivists and the general public.

A major objective of national libraries is to provide easy access to the wealth of information resources that reside in libraries and other cultural institutions in that country. To achieve this, the libraries maintain websites that provide information about library policies, collections and services. These websites also provide access to electronic resources and databases on the Internet.

Services to Libraries and Other Collecting Institutions
National libraries facilitate nationwide and worldwide access to information to, and from, libraries in their country. These services are available to all libraries regardless of their size or client base, and allow them to share in the globalization of information provision.

The Library of Congress's work on enhancing cataloging services has been made available globally via the LC online catalog, and through the Library's worldwide cataloging distribution service. These national bibliographic resources have millions of entries for books, serials and items such as films, sound and video recordings, maps, pictures, CDs, braille and talking books, music scores, and electronic journals.

National Bibliographies
National bibliographies record the works of, or about, one country. Most printed bibliographies have been replaced by integrated catalog systems, networks and databases, enabling one country's publications to be selected during a search. These searches can be limited by subject and/or timeframe to produce a selection of documents relevant to a particular user's needs.

Services to the Public
In general, anyone can use a national library's public reading rooms. National libraries deliver an extensive range of services to users onsite and through their websites.

Many users, particularly researchers, reach the limits of the resources in their own libraries. The national library complements and extends the services offered to them by other libraries. Provision is often made for scholars using a national library to store the material they are using over a long period.

Promotion
National libraries promote their activities and collections in a variety of ways, including exhibitions, publications, events and education programs.

Preservation
A national library plays an important role in preserving its country's documentary heritage, and making sure it is available for people to use for as long as possible into the future. The aim of preservation services is to maintain and preserve items according to their use and their significance.

International Activities

National libraries support other libraries and similar agencies. They usually belong to international organizations concerned with the development of libraries and information services. They maintain a significant presence in the international library and research community through organizations such as IFLA (International Federation of Library Associations and Institutions). Regionally, they may also assist less developed countries with training, preservation activities and the provision of funds for the purchase of books and equipment.

EXERCISE 11.1

Go to websites of two of the following national libraries and compare their services with those provided by the Library of Congress at http://www.loc.gov.

British Library at http://www.bl.uk/

National Library of Australia at http://www.nla.gov.au

National Library of New Zealand at http://www.natlib.govt.nz/

National Library of Canada at http://www.collectionscanada.ca/

EXERCISE 11.2

Go to the National Agricultural Library's website at <http://www.nal.usda.gov/> and answer the following questions.

1. Give the title of one item included in 'Agricultural Education' which is located under the 'Education and Outreach' section of 'Topics'.

2. What is the topic of the latest exhibition at the National Agricultural Library?

3. What is DigiTop? How can it be accessed and by whom?

4. Name two agricultural 'Information centers' mentioned on the website.

5. What is one of the special collections held by the National Agricultural Library? What types of resources are held in this collection?

6. What information products for rural information needs are available on the website?

State Libraries

A state library is funded by a state or territory to provide library services to the whole state, including support to the public libraries in the state.

The State Library of New South Wales, in Australia, is one example. It holds over 5 million items (including monographs, pictures, posters, ephemera, sheet music, talking books, maps, CD-ROMs, newspapers, microfilm and fiche, films and videos, computer software, kits, sound recordings, photographs, objects, architectural plans, coins and postage stamps). The Library offers advice and support to local councils providing public library services to the people of New South Wales. This includes consultancy and advice on collection management and local studies library services. It also provides funding to NSW councils through subsidies and grants. The Mitchell Library holds research materials in Australia's history, culture and literature.

The State Library of Louisiana is another example. Its collections include books, magazines, newspapers, state and federal government documents and audiovisual materials. The Louisiana Section houses a comprehensive collection of information about Louisiana, including books about the state, books by Louisiana authors, Louisiana periodicals, historical documents, maps, photographs, and much more. The library's services for the blind and physically handicapped provides books and magazines in large-print, braille and recorded formats to residents who are unable to use conventional reading materials.

In some countries, including Australia and Denmark, legal deposit legislation also applies at the state level. This means that publishers must deposit a copy of every item published in that state into the state library, as well as the national library. This contributes immensely to the resources of state libraries. They also house important historical collections relating to the development of their states.

State libraries have developed services for their state communities that complement and extend the role of the country's national library. These include extensive reference services and specialist business information services, advisory units for conservation, extensive photographic collections, and resources and access to specialist community groups (e.g., indigenous communities, people with disabilities, and members of multicultural communities).

State libraries have a role in the development and support of public libraries, ranging from consultative functions to stocking and staffing libraries, as well as establishing electronic networks with the public libraries to extend their range of services. Some of their services have been established as commercial operations, while their basic library services are free to members of the public.

Clients include the public, other libraries, the business community and researchers.

EXERCISE 11.3

Locate the web page of your state, territory, provincial or county library.

1. Does legal deposit legislation apply to your state library? If so, what can you find out about it? If your state does not have legal deposit legislation, find a state library near you that does and explain how it works.

2. List the range of services offered. Indicate if any of these services are commercially-based.

Public Libraries

A public library is funded by federal, state and/or local government taxes. Public libraries provide library services to all sections of the community.

Public libraries provide services to people who live, work or are educated in the same area, serving the information needs of all members of the community. For many people it is the only library to which they have access. Services are available to individuals or to members of a particular group. Users include adults, children, young adults, the homebound, the institutionalized, the isolated, ethnic groups, people with disabilities, local government, clubs, societies and small businesses.

UNESCO's Public Library Manifesto describes the public library "as a living force for education, culture and information, and is an essential agent for the fostering of peace and spiritual welfare through the minds of men and women."
www.unesco.org/webworld/libraries/manifestos/libraman.html

Objectives
The objectives of public libraries are:
- recreational—reading, listening, viewing
- informational—helping people in their day-to-day living
- vocational—a source of information for vocational and continuing education
- educational—a source of resources for people's life-long education

- advisory—information about community, local, regional, state and national activities
- referral—suggesting the best sources of information if the library cannot supply them.

Types of Public Library

Municipal/Council/Local

Municipal or local public libraries are generally established by local government authorities and maintained from local or state taxes. Subsidies may involve cash or kind, based on the size of the population, and matching local government expenditure. These libraries respond to local needs and requests, and may service populations with small branch libraries or with mobile libraries (sometimes known as bookmobiles).

Regional

Regional library services are established by agreement between several local government authorities. This approach may be adopted because of sparse population or shortage of funds.

Joint-Use Libraries

A joint-use library serves two or more different groups of users, usually involving public and education libraries, or public and state libraries.

EXERCISE 11.4

Some services are unique to public libraries. In the list below circle the library services you consider are unique to public libraries.

loans

interlibrary loan

reference

Internet access

community information

literacy support

local history

children's services (e.g., storytelling, holiday activities)

extension services to remote users, housebound, aged, hospital patients

access to foreign language collections

access to large print and talking books

displays - in-house or from local organizations, schools

access to CDs, videos, prints

booklists (e.g., new books, subjects)

award celebrations (e.g., Children's Book Week)

clubs for various users

bookmobiles

Collections

Public libraries may have separate sections for children, young adults and adults, or the sections may be combined. The holdings include a range of materials in scope, readership, subject matter and format. Types of material include fiction, non-fiction, reference, periodicals, DVDs, audio- and videocassettes, CDs, records, films, toys and maps. Some public libraries even provide tools, posters and pictures to meet their clients' needs, and others offer used books for sale at bargain prices. These sales are often run by Friends of the Library.

Public library collections are influenced by the location of the library (e.g., a large foreign language collection will develop in an area with a large ethnic population). Libraries need to develop selection policies that address the needs of local users, and are flexible enough to accommodate new user groups, changing information needs and new formats.

Specifically, public libraries need a policy regarding the purchase of popular fiction titles (e.g., restricting purchase to paperback editions). They also need a policy for handling donations that may be inappropriate, take up too much space, or do not fit the collection guidelines.

Public libraries usually use Dewey Decimal Classification to classify their collections. This classification scheme reflects the wide subject coverage of a public library collection.

Promotion of Library Services

Public relations are important to public libraries. The library staff aim to increase the use of the library, and encourage non-users to become involved. If the level of use increases, the level of funding is more likely to be increased, and the library will be able to expand its services. It is necessary to make the community aware of the library and its services in order to justify the expense of providing the library.

EXERCISE 11.5

List ways in which a public library may promote its services.

Issues Faced by Public Libraries
Public library concerns include:
- keeping up with technological developments (e.g., Internet, e-books)
- meeting a wide range of needs and expectations
- maintaining free core services
- coping with staffing and financial constraints
- the increasing cost of resources
- censorship issues
- competition from DVDs and television
- rationalization, amalgamation and competitive tendering of service
- multiethnic populations.

Joint-Use Libraries
In a joint-use library, two or more distinct groups of users are served with equal priority in the same premises, the governance of which is cooperatively arranged between two or more separate authorities.

Joint-use libraries are sometimes known as community libraries. They are usually shared between a public library and a primary, secondary or tertiary educational institution.

Aims and Objectives
A joint-use library aims to provide a better level of library service than would be possible in two separate facilities. It provides resources and services to meet:
- the information needs of the community and the educational institution
- the formal and informal educational needs of the community and the educational institution
- the cultural and recreational needs of all its users.

It provides a cost-effective library service for the community by:
- rationalizing resources
- eliminating duplication of scarce and expensive material
- maximizing availability and use of resources and services
- providing access to library networks of various kinds.

Issues for Joint-Use Libraries
- *Access:* In order to operate efficiently, a joint-use library should be accessible in every sense to all its users. It needs a convenient location in relation to other community facilities. Whenever possible, all materials should be accessible by all users, but problems may occur with project material or short loan items. If located in a school building, the service may need separate entrances for the public and for the school community. There should be no restrictions on use by the public during school or college class times.
- *Planning:* All parties need to be involved in planning, but problems may arise if the joint-use library is established in an existing single-purpose library facility.

- *Finance:* Problems may arise concerning who pays for the facilities, resources and staff.
- *Provision of resources:* The participating services have to decide whether the collection is integrated into one sequence or divided according to user group.
- *Management and staffing:* A hierarchy of decision-making should be established to facilitate effective administration.

Activity 11.6

Many libraries impose fines for overdue material, to encourage users to return items on time, thus making them available for other users.

Here are some arguments made for and against fines. Can you think of more?

In favour of fines	Against fines
Users will return material on time to avoid a fine	Fines are bad for public relations
Fines are a source of income	Ratepayers feel that they have already paid for a library service
The collection should be readily available to all users and anything overdue is out of circulation	Some borrowers may never return loans if they have to pay fines
	Procedures for enforcing payment are time-consuming

Academic Libraries

An academic library serves the staff and students of a tertiary institution such as a university or college, and reflects the instructional and research programs conducted at that institution.

The major categories of users are academic staff, both teachers and researchers; undergraduate students, both on and off campus; postgraduate students; and administrative staff.

Many academic libraries also allow other users to access their collections by paying a fee, or belong to schemes that allow reciprocal borrowing.

Academic institutions often undergo great changes, experiencing expansion, amalgamations and rationalization. Libraries in academic institutions can also experience these changes, from holding decentralized collections servicing certain faculties or clusters, to becoming large centralized units, or vice versa. All academic libraries deal with changes in teaching methods, such as off-campus learning, open universities and flexible learning. Electronic technology has helped academic libraries to deliver information differently to staff and students.

Objectives
Academic libraries aim to:
- educate and assist students and staff in the use of information resources
- provide current library resources and databases that support the academic curriculum
- provide access to information resources, regardless of the location of the user.

Collections
- Collections cover a wide variety of subjects based on the curricula, and libraries need to adapt to new developments in curriculum.
- Many universities emphasize research, but there are also requirements to provide basic texts over many subject areas.
- Academic libraries have strong non-book collections (e.g., electronic books and journals, microforms, DVDs).
- Academic libraries increasingly rely on electronic media to satisfy information needs.

Services to Users
- Academic libraries emphasize user assistance and instruction in the use of their resources. Since students use the library extensively for several years, they need to be familiar with the catalog, reference sources and online resources. The academic staff also need to be aware of the library's services. Some faculties (e.g., law) require their students to be formally trained in accessing information. This may become the responsibility of the library.
- Researchers and academic staff need to be well informed about developments in their fields, so the library aims to provide current awareness services and journal circulation.

- Users have different needs. While undergraduates need standard texts, audiovisual material and material for short loan, postgraduates and academic staff need advanced material, periodical literature and even primary material for research and teaching.
- There is heavy use of electronic reference sources.
- Library staff instruct users on search techniques.
- Sophisticated circulation systems are required to cope with the large turnover of resources, different categories of borrowers and differing loan periods.
- Sophisticated reserve systems, called Short Loan, Reserve or Closed Reserve, are necessary because of the high demand for some material:
  o Loans may be for 1 or 2 hours, overnight or 1 or 2 days.
  o Multiple copies of resources may be required to meet the demand.
  o Ensuring efficient use of the collection requires constant supervision.
  o Library staff liaise with academic staff who recommend material for short loan.
  o Material may include texts, photocopies, tapes and transcripts of lectures, audiovisual material, lecturers' private copies.
  o If an item is reserved frequently, it will be relocated in short loan.
- Detailed statistics are kept to measure usage of the short loan collection.
- Photocopying and computer facilities are provided to students.
- Interlibrary loans are available to academic staff and researchers.
- Academic libraries may have arrangements with similar institutions for students to have reciprocal borrowing rights, thus increasing user access to information sources.

Digital Repositories

Digital repositories are online archives that collect, preserve, and disseminate digital resources that have been produced by the academic staff and students. They may be subject-based or institutional in their focus. They can include a wide range of content for a variety of purposes and users, including research outputs such as journal articles or research data, e-theses, e-learning objects and teaching materials, and administrative data. Some repositories only accept specific items (such as theses or journal articles), while others gather any scholarly work produced by the institution.

An institutional digital repository might also include other digital resources generated by academics, such as administrative documents, course notes, learning objects, or conference proceedings. Deposit of material in an institutional repository is sometimes mandated by that institution.

Some of the main objectives for having a digital repository are to:
- provide open access to institutional research output
- create global visibility for an institution's scholarly research
- store and preserve other digital resources, including unpublished or otherwise easily lost grey literature such as theses or technical reports.

Library staff may have responsibility for adding subject analysis to the resources held in digital repositories. They may also be given jurisdiction over copyright implications attached to resources held in the repository.

Open Access Libraries

Open access libraries hold resources that are made available electronically, free of charge with unrestricted access via the Internet, usually under a Creative Commons Licence. The resources can be made available through archives, repositories and open access journals.

Currently, there are three forms of open access:
- *Green Open Access*: A research article that has been accepted for publication in a scholarly journal is freely available online to readers. This is because the author has archived a full-text copy of it in an institutional or subject repository.
- *Gold Open Access*: The publisher of a scholarly journal provides free online access to the full content of the journal. Sometimes the publisher charges the author an article processing fee, other times the costs are covered by subsidies from institutions and scholarly societies. Gold Open Access may also occur when the journal is freely available online after a delayed period of time.
- *Hybrid Open Access*: Immediate open access is provided to individual papers in subscription-based journals when the author pays a fee for their article to be freely available online. As institutions also pay to subscribe to the journal, some institutions consider this is 'double-dipping'.

There are a number of benefits to open access, including:
- allowing anyone to view an article without having to pay
- increasing the impact of an article. By reaching more readers, the potential for more citations improves (which may also increase the credibility of the journal that published it)
- speeding up the sharing of results with other researchers who could build on it and practitioners who could apply the new knowledge
- access to a greater number of scholarly journals
- opportunities to highlight research outputs.

Virtual Educational Institutions

Virtual educational institutions provide higher education programs through electronic media. The term encompasses corporate training centers, individual institutional distance learning initiatives, non-profit and government education activities, as well as state and multistate higher learning collaborations.

Some virtual educational institutions are physical institutions that provide online learning as part of their extended courses while others solely offer online courses. They are regarded as a form of distance education.

The goal of virtual educational institutions is to provide access to tertiary education to those who are not able to attend a physical campus, possibly because of distance or the need for flexibility in their study program. Students of these institutions may live anywhere in the world. Examples of virtual educational institutions include 'African Virtual University' (http://www.avu.org/), 'Virtual University of Pakistan' (http://www.vu.edu.pk/) and the Canadian Virtual University (http://www.cvu-uvc.ca/), to name just a few.

Some universities that are virtual institutions also have virtual libraries which aim to support the academic rigours of their students in the same ways as other academic libraries.

Issues for Academic Libraries

The following issues are of particular concern to all types of academic libraries:
- extended opening hours to cater for the needs of users
- providing wireless networks that allow students to work anywhere, on or off campus
- the cost of keeping up with technology
- the storage of electronic information
- a large interlibrary loan burden
- the cost of resourcing new courses
- copyright considerations
- lack of storage space
- the need to provide study space as well as storage for the collection
- the need for, and the expense of, security systems
- the problem of penalties for overdue material such as fines and restricted borrowing
- budgeting for demand-driven acquisitions (that are paid for on a per-usage arrangement).

ACTIVITY 11.7

Locate the home page of an academic library and note the services provided by that library. Note the electronic resources that are available to clients, with and without passwords.

School Libraries

A school library serves the students and staff in a school. The library provides resources for the use of its students—for recreational reading, and for research purposes relevant to the curriculum. It also holds resources that staff use in developing and teaching courses.

Clients include students, teachers and parents.

Objectives
A school library aims to:
- provide resources to meet the needs of the staff, and students
- provide resources to support the development and teaching of courses
- direct students towards correct library use
- encourage reading.

School libraries are often the first real contact children have with libraries and good literature. A school library should aim to interest and challenge a child in developing reading skills. School students should be taught how to locate information during library lessons, and encouraged to undertake independent study or research.

Learning Resource Center
Most school libraries include non-print resources such as kits, puppets, models, construction sets and teaching aids. They may house and distribute class sets of texts and reading sets, as well as multimedia equipment. These diverse materials and formats result in school libraries often being described as learning resource centers.

The Teacher-Librarian
A school librarian has a dual role:
- to select, evaluate and organize materials to assist in the teaching program and to meet the educational, recreational and cultural needs of the school community
- to cooperate with teachers and guide students in developing the best ways of using the resources available to achieve the aims of the teaching program and to develop the students' information literacy.

Teacher-librarians usually have library qualifications as well as teaching qualifications.

Collections
A school library should provide:
- up-to-date reference materials for teachers and students
- materials at appropriate reading levels to meet the need for:
    - research information
    - reading for pleasure
    - hobbies and interests
    - current awareness.

The collection should include:
- latest editions of standard reference works
- recent non-fiction books
- fiction
- picture books (for younger children)
- newspapers and periodicals
- pamphlets
- DVDs
- games, toys (for younger children)
- educational models
- equipment such as laptops and DVD players
- educational CD-ROMs
- word processing packages.

Collection Development
- There is an emphasis on supporting the curriculum and encouraging teachers to be involved in the selection process.
- School libraries increasingly use multimedia material particularly for teaching.
- Keeping up with developments in children's literature is essential for teacher-librarians.

There is seldom enough room to keep infrequently used items, so school libraries need to weed frequently and dispose of unused or outdated material. A small, relevant collection is more likely to be used than a large, uncontrolled one.

Services
School libraries offer:
- reference service and assistance to students
- individual instruction and classes in library use
- loans
- facilities for making or playing DVD recordings
- guidance in reading
- book clubs
- children's book week celebrations
- staff consultation with teachers
- online databases
- CD-ROMs and Internet access
- document delivery of articles
- photocopying.

Issues for School Libraries

- *Funding:* Lack of funds to supply and build up collections has been a major concern for school libraries. Many schools have to rely on fundraising by parents. They may also take advantage of book club purchase plans where the school library receives a percentage in cash or kind of material bought by the school community.
- *Staffing:* Teacher-librarians often rely on assistance from older students and parents because of insufficient support staff. Some schools are not able to employ a teacher-librarian or other staff member with library training; in these cases, a teacher or teacher's assistant coordinates the library.
- *Space:* Many school libraries are poorly located (e.g., in a surplus classroom) which may discourage use.
- *Status:* The school library is often seen as a 'child-minding center' or the teacher-librarian is called upon to fill staffing gaps when other staff are away. The important information role of the library is not always supported by other staff in the school.
- *Collection development:* It can often be difficult to find materials to support new subjects at the appropriate level, especially if the librarian has not been given enough prior notification of curriculum developments.

Cooperation with Public Libraries

School and public librarians need to cooperate to avoid duplication of materials and programs. Both play a vital role in providing information services to children, and they should complement each other. Consultation about programs and curricula benefits both parties. Joint use libraries are an example of successful cooperation.

ACTIVITY 11.8

Locate the home page of two school libraries and compare the services they provide to their school community. Note what information literacy information is provided by the library staff.

Special Libraries

A special library:
- collects in a limited subject area
- is usually attached to a society, institution, association, government department, public utility or commercial organization. The subject field is determined by the interests of the body maintaining it.

Special libraries exist in all areas of private, government and community enterprise. These libraries may also be known as 'corporate' libraries.

Special libraries usually have a limited number of users with a specified aim. The users are staff of the organization, and their special needs include:
- detailed information from a specific subject field
- up-to-date information provided promptly.

Special libraries vary in size, sometimes proportional to the size of the organization and at other times dependent on the use made by staff within the organization. Special libraries can be impacted by the way that staff support the library. Therefore, the library's importance is often dependent on its users and their position within the organization's structure.

Objectives

Special libraries aim to:
- provide information in support of the objectives of their parent body
- save time and effort on the part of the staff of the organization who need exact information for their work. The information is often complex and required urgently
- be proactive and anticipate requests for information.

ACTIVITY 11.9

List examples of special libraries in the table below.

Type of Special Library	Examples
Government department/agency	
Professional association/organization	
Company/business	
Subject-specific (e.g., law, theology, music)	
Resource-specific (e.g., braille, film, newspaper)	

Collections
- Resources in the collection are determined by the role of the parent organization.
- Collections are often small but comprehensive in certain subject areas and types of resources.
- Special libraries seldom have the space or the need to keep material that is not currently in use.
- Emphasis is on providing up-to-date information rather than historical information, but some special libraries have a small archival function, keeping in-house material.
- As well as books and journals, the collection may include reports, specifications, memoranda, unpublished papers, etc.
- There is a growing dependence on electronic sources of information, including commercial databases, the Internet, electronic journals and computer-aided design (CAD) software.
- There is heavy reliance on the use of networks and cooperative agreements to widen the scope of the collections.

Acquisition
- Selection needs to keep pace with changes in the research program of the parent organization.
- The users are seen as subject experts. They are asked to evaluate the library's selection policy and suggest purchases based on their expertise. There is often a library committee that oversees subject suggestions and offers advice to the library.

Circulation
Special libraries often have a casual approach to loans. Users may check out their own loans, have permanent loans and maintain collections in their offices. Many special libraries are open after normal working hours for their clients, and rely on the clients to record their own loans. All these arrangements impact on the provision of interlibrary loans to other libraries, since much time can be spent locating an item.

Cataloging and Classification
Bibliographic control is usually tailored to the library's needs. Subject cataloging may be very complex, with many detailed, specific subject headings. These may be determined by a specialist subject thesaurus, or an in-house thesaurus developed for the organization.

The need for subject control sometimes leads to the use of specialist classification schemes such as Universal Decimal Classification (UDC) and Moys Classification (for law libraries). In small special libraries, classification systems for shelf arrangements are often developed inhouse.

Public Services
Special libraries are not open to the general public but when providing services to their staff they provide:
- answers to complex reference enquiries
- loans and interlibrary loans
- current awareness services

- compilation of bibliographies in anticipation of demand or on request
- direct access to electronic journals, or circulation of periodicals or contents pages
- new acquisitions lists
- displays of new books and journals
- newspaper cutting services
- indexing and abstracting of serial literature (inhouse or commercial)
- online searching
- RSS feeds
- library bulletins
* information analysis
* audiovisual copying.

The emphasis in these libraries is on getting current, relevant information to users. The library staff are more likely to undertake research on behalf of their users. They often anticipate users' requests, rather than wait for users to initiate requests.

Issues for Special Libraries
* There is a need to prove cost-effectiveness, to retain funds, resources and space.
* The library may be overlooked in the hierarchy of the organization.
* The librarian often reports to non-library-oriented management: for example, being located with the information technology section or records management section.
* Special libraries are often found in non-traditional settings and inconvenient housing, such as offices or basements.
* Collections may be moved to offsite warehouse storage and individual resources delivered on request.
* Special government libraries often face problems with being restructured and reorganized.
* Government libraries must meet government requirements to provide metadata for their organization's websites.
* There is often a lack of trained staff to provide adequate access to the collection.

CHAPTER TWELVE
Library Networks

Introduction
A network is:
- two or more libraries or other organizations, often of a similar type, which exchange information
- a group of organizations able and willing to collaborate to improve library-based information services.

The term 'network' can refer to:
- hardware
- software
- projects
- agencies
- communication systems
- materials
- services.

Why do Libraries Join Networks?
Libraries join networks:
- to improve services to specific target populations
- because libraries can no longer be self-sufficient in terms of their collections, personnel or services
- to save time, money and effort
- to gain access to more information in an effort to cope with the 'information explosion'
- to gain from the experience of other libraries by exchanging information and expertise.

Reasons for Not Joining a Network
Some libraries are reluctant to join networks because:
- the cost can be high for minimal benefit
- cooperation is not seen as important
- they are satisfied with local services
- their collections may contain confidential material
- small libraries may be overwhelmed with service demands
- members of the network have conflicting policies
- they fear losing their autonomy.

The advancement of computer technology has greatly assisted the development of networks because it allows libraries to share bibliographic data easily. It provides extended access to sources of information over vast geographical distances, and facilitates communication between members of the network.

Range of Cooperation
Libraries may cooperate by:
- sharing a catalog and database in order to help each member library catalog its own resources
- creating union catalogs to facilitate interlibrary loans and document delivery
- developing a joint acquisitions policy
- exchanging bibliographic data
- sharing storage facilities
- buying materials and/or equipment cooperatively to save funds
- arranging reciprocal borrowing for their users
- participating in interlibrary lending.

Types of Networks
- Networks can be formal or informal depending on the size of the library and its requirements.
- A library may belong to several networks depending on its differing needs.
- Networks may be international, national, regional, local or subject-related.

International Networks
The Internet has made it easier for international networks to exist and to be used as many formal networks use the Internet to facilitate their own operations. Most organizations and groups use the Internet to promote themselves and to provide access to their resources through their website.

OCLC (Online Computer Library Center)
OCLC (http://www.oclc.org) , a US-based consortium, is a nonprofit computer library service and research organization. More than 72,000 libraries in 170 countries and territories around the world use OCLC services to locate, acquire, catalog, lend or preserve library materials.

Services include *WorldCat* (the OCLC online union catalog), cataloging services, and the maintenance and administration of Dewey Decimal Classification. OCLC also provides reference services though *FirstSearch,* as well as a large interlibrary loans network.

INASP (International Network for the Availability of Scientific Publications)
INASP (http://www.inasp.info/) is a cooperative network established in 1992 that aims to strengthen and promote access to, and dissemination of, scholarly information between and within countries. INASP offers free or low-cost access to scholarly journals to institutions in

the developing world, to assist them in solving their development challenges. They work with 21 partner countries and over 80 network countries around the world.

HINARI (Health InterNetwork Access to Research Initiative)
HINARI (http://www.who.int/hinari/en/) is a World Health Organization initiative to strengthen public health services by providing public health workers, researchers and policymakers with access to high-quality, relevant and timely health information. It does this by improving access to the major journals in biomedical and related social sciences to public institutions in developing countries. 170 publisher partners, and up to a further 400 publishers, currently offer more than 51,000 information resources in HINARI. Free access is supplied to 72 countries and a further 44 countries are provided with low cost access.

National Networks
Many national libraries around the world maintain large national networks that are known as national union catalogs. A national union catalog is an automated national bibliographic and information network, based on a cooperative online shared cataloging facility. The primary function of catalog networks is to facilitate shared cataloging. When libraries describe their resources in a standardized way (using descriptive cataloging guidelines such as RDA) and encode them in a standard communication format (such as MARC) they are able to share their bibliographic records with other libraries. Sharing bibliographic records is common when one library buys a resource that has already been obtained and described by another library. Using catalog records already available from a union catalog eliminates duplication by allowing records to be copied. This is called copy cataloging.

Cataloging networks also support interlibrary loan arrangements between participants. Interlibrary loan systems work best when libraries use union catalogs that are current (new titles are added regularly and withdrawn titles are removed promptly) and full of standardized, accurate information.

Cataloging Services
The Library of Congress, AMICUS, OCLC, the British National Bibliography, Libraries Australia, New Zealand's Te Puna and many others provide online cataloging, searching and downline loading. Original cataloging and other associated records are created online in real time. Once a record has been input, it is available immediately for ordering, and for other users to view.

Interlibrary Loan (ILL)/Document Delivery
Document delivery services allow libraries to:
- search union catalogs or national bibliographic databases for records
- create requests and automatically include bibliographic and location data from the source library
- select suppliers that may be close at hand
- track requests
- use the ILL payment and delivery schemes.

State Networks

Where they exist, state networks are usually, but not always, a collaboration of the state library (or another significant library), and public libraries within that state. Under the coordination of the major library, network participants access services that would normally be too expensive for each library to use individually. State networks may also provide:
- interlibrary loan services
- document delivery services
- database services
- online newspapers
- electronic access to libraries' catalogs
- research services.

Examples include:
- CAVAL (http://www.caval.edu.au/), a consortium of academic libraries in Australia
- Maine School and Library Network (MSLN) (http://msln.net/), a consortium of school and public libraries across the state of Maine through which participants acquire Internet access and library services
- OhioLINK, Ohio Library & Information Network (http://www.ohiolink.edu/content/), a state-funded consortium of 90 college and university libraries, plus the State Library of Ohio
- South Australian Public Library Network (http://www.libraries.sa.gov.au/) operates within an agreement between the state and local governments.

Local and Regional Networks

There are many formal and informal networks based on location. A number of libraries in a city or region allow each other free interlibrary loans, share resources, provide training and refer clients to other libraries in the network. These may be special libraries, school or public libraries working together. Examples include:
- Eastern Regional Libraries (http://www.erl.vic.gov.au/) is a co-operative venture between the public libraries of three councils—Knox, Maroondah and Yarra Ranges—in Victoria, Australia.
- Glasgow Academic Libraries Together (GALT) (http://www.slainte.org.uk/galt/) aims to develop cooperation and knowledge sharing between the academic and city libraries of the greater Glasgow area of Scotland.
- Heartland Regional Library Network (HRLN) (http://www.heartlandlibraries.org/) is a network of public, academic, school and special libraries in California in the USA.
- Northern New York Library Network (NNYLN) (http://www.nnyln.org/) facilitates cooperative services among the libraries in northern New York and seeks to improve library services within the region.
- Shorelink (http://www.shorelink.nsw.gov.au/) is a network of five public libraries on the North Shore of Sydney in Australia, which share a common infrastructure to maximize service to their communities.
- Southern Ontario Library Service (SOLS) (http://www.sols.org/) is a network that connects 149 public libraries and one university in Southern Ontario, Canada, providing equitable access to library services.

Subject-Related Networks

Libraries within specific subject areas, including criminology, health/medicine, law, and military services, have formed networks to provide each other with free interlibrary loan services and wider access to information. Other libraries form networks because of common governance, such as government libraries.

For example:
- AGLIN (http://www.aglin.org/), Australian Government Libraries Information Network, delivers information services to Australian Government organizations.
- MERLN (http://ndu.libguides.com/merln) Military Education Research Library Network is a consortium of military education research libraries in the United States.
- National Network of Libraries of Medicine (NN/LM) (http://nnlm.gov/) advances the progress of medicine and improving public health in the United States through access to health information.
- NELLCO, Inc. (http://www.nellco.org/), is an international consortium of law libraries, including academic, state, court and county, and private non-profit law libraries in the United States, Canada, the United Kingdom, and Australia.
- World Criminal Justice Library Electronic Network (WCJLN) (http://andromeda.rutgers.edu/~wcjlen/WCJ/) develops ways of sharing services and criminal justice information on a global scale.

EXERCISE 12.1

Locate the home pages of two library networks on the Internet and write down the aims and membership information of each network.

CHAPTER THIRTEEN
Other Information Agencies

Introduction
In Chapters 10-12 we chose libraries as a type of information agency, and examined the library's functions in detail. However, many other organizations act as information providers. This chapter introduces a range of information agencies, and the information professions related to them. It discusses the types of records found in, and used by, records management agencies and archives, and outlines the roles and functions of other information agencies.

Types of Information Agencies
The following types of agencies provide, store and preserve information:
- libraries
- archives
- museums
- art galleries
- resource centers
- registries
- community information agencies
- records management sections
- information technology units
- tourist bureaus
- sections of government departments (e.g., Social Security, Consumer Affairs, Public Relations)
- citizens' advice bureaus
- welfare organizations (e.g., National Suicide Prevention Lifeline)
- embassies
- lobby groups (e.g., National Farmers Union, National Organization for Women (NOW))
- non-government organizations (NGOs) (e.g., World Vision, Greenpeace, CARE)
- electronic information providers (e.g., the Internet, bulletin boards, blogs, chat groups, listservs).

Providers of Information
The following people are interested in the use of information and providing the right information to the right person at the right time:

information worker	information officer
information analyst	information manager
librarian	library technician
archivist	webmaster
research officer	records manager
indexer	bibliographer
curator of art gallery, museum etc.	knowledge manager

Several groups of professionals deal with information at different stages of its active or inactive life:
- Librarians chiefly deal with published material in a variety of formats.
- Records managers handle semi-active or active documents.
- Archivists manage inactive records.
- Community information workers, often volunteers, distribute verbal and written information to community information seekers.

Theory of Three Ages of Documents

This diagram illustrates the evolution of documents from their creation to their destruction or permanent storage. This is known as the life cycle of documents. It processes documents through three stages: active, semi-active and inactive. At each stage, the documents are the concern of a different information professional.

Personnel	Stage	Proportion
Staff and administrative personnel	**Creation of documents**	100% of documents
Records managers or clerical staff	**Active documents** • maximum primary value • kept in registry office for immediate referral	some documents eliminated

Records managers	**Semi-active documents**
	• primary value
	  - reduced
	  - weak
	  - nil
	• some secondary value
		some documents eliminated

Archivists	**Inactive documents** • transfer to archives • maximum secondary value	5%-10% of all documents created

Records Management

Records management is regarded as the systematic control of corporate or government correspondence from creation to final disposal. It focuses on procedures and systems for the storage, retrieval and disposal of an organization's records.

Records management systems are necessary because organizations rely on efficient access to the right information or 'corporate record':
- to support decision-making
- for operational purposes
- as evidence of policies and activities
- for support in case of litigation.

Organizations are legally required to create certain records and to retain certain categories of records for specified purposes and specified time periods. Some examples of these types of records are tax files, personnel records, or records to comply with stock exchange requirements.

Organizations need to devise systems to collect, store and control the volume of paper and electronic documents.

Records management systems include policies for retention and disposal of records, and for the separation of active and semi-active records. Some records can then be transferred to archives. Records managers deal largely with current information of primary value to the organization. Archivists are concerned with the long term historical and research value of the organization's documentation. Retention times vary with the institutions and its mandate.

Categories of Records

In most records management units, records can be categorized into:
- administrative (policy and procedure manuals, organizational charts)
- correspondence (emails, memos and letters, often registered and retained in registry sections)
- transactional records (which could include invoices and accounts)
- project records
- case files
- personnel files
- historical (minutes of meetings, public relations documents).

Record Management Terms

Some of the more frequently used technical terms and their meanings as used by records managers are explained in the following table.

Classification	The process by which files and documents are categorized or grouped to facilitate retrieval. This system usually reflects the internal working structure of the organization and the chronology of the records.
Indexing	Assigning search elements, terms or labels to enable users to retrieve needed items.
Records disposal	Transfer of records from active to inactive storage (e.g., an archive); destruction of unwanted records
Records retention and disposal schedule	A list of the records of an organization with directions for how they are to be disposed of after their creation and initial use.
Retention period	The specific time period for which records are kept before they are destroyed.
Sentencing	Deciding where and for how long records should be kept.
Thesaurus	An alphabetical listing (usually subject related) of allowed and non-allowed terms, by which records are categorized.

Archives

Archives are collections of records or historical documents that are preserved permanently because of their enduring interest or value. The works in archives are generally items that have not been published.

Value of Archives

Archives meet the needs of clients by supplying original source documents. These include:
- records as evidence - this is the fundamental reason to keep archives. The aim is to be able to re-create the activities of an individual or institution objectively and authentically through study of original documents.
- administrative uses - the secondary value of documents, as these documents can be referred to in relation to current issues.
- reconstruction - used for historical investigation and research.

Types of Records Collected by Archives

The following types of records are collected and stored:

files	working papers	correspondence
memoranda	pamphlets	invoices
newsreels	films	drawings
models	plans	charts
paintings	posters	sound recordings
videos	photographs	computer printouts
electronic records	technical reports	diaries (usually official)
(magnetic tapes, discs)	CDs	DVDs
USB drives	digital communications	intranets and websites

Archival Principles

Two principles are the basis of archival organization: provenance, and respect for the original order.

Provenance

The source of the material must be respected, and it is important not to interfile records of different institutions or individuals. A group of records continues to reflect the history and planning of that institution or individual, even if that institution or person no longer exists. The material from those sources must be respected by continuing to treat each source as an entity.

Respect the Original Order

The order in which an organization or individual created, maintained and used records should be respected and preserved, even if it is disorganized and haphazard. How the material is organized reveals the way the institution functioned or the personnel organized their work.

Storing Archives

Archives are stored in a building called a repository. It is often specially designed to include airconditioning, air-filtering and humidity control but to exclude light in order to maintain the records in good condition. Boxes for archiving files and papers must be of archival quality, or acid free.

Types of Records

Local Government Records

The value of these archives and records is now recognized and much work is being done to find and preserve these invaluable sources of information. Historical societies have often done most work to preserve local records. These old records are often literally pulled out of musty basements and rescued by local historians. Many public libraries are now repositories for local government archives.

Non-Government Records
All commercial organizations create records of value to themselves, and many produce records that have research value for others. Their records can be valuable as a source of social, economic, scientific, and technical information.

Non-commercial enterprises, including educational institutions, hospitals, religious bodies, trade unions, and political organizations, are major producers and users of information. Their records also need proper management, as some of them are archival in character.

Many commercial and non-commercial organizations have developed records management programs, and have established respositories. Some have handed their archives to other institutions. Universities have shown a greater appreciation of archives than other kinds of organizations. Many universities, for example, have not only developed repositories for their own archives, but also solicit archival materials from commercial enterprises, other institutions and organizations, and individuals, because they constitute a valuable research resource for faculty and students.

National Archives
Many national archives began as part of national or state library collections, and were separated out when archives authorities were established. Occasionally the reverse has happened—e.g., the Public Archives of Canada joined with the newer National Library of Canada to become Library and Archives Canada (http://www.bac-lac.gc.ca/eng/) in 2004.

National archives hold records relating to government departments and statutory authorities, commissions and committees of inquiry. They also hold records created individually by politicians and bureaucrats. National archive agencies are involved in all aspects of information control of federal government documentation systems, from creation to selection decisions on what material is valuable enough to be archived. Holdings are many and varied, consisting of files (hard copies and electronic), films, maps, microforms, photographs, paintings and realia. A notable example is the piano of Glenn Gould, international musical icon, that is housed in Library and Archives Canada.

Functions of National Archives
In order to meet the various needs of governments and the public, national archives are governed by specific legislation. They are usually mandated to:
- identify government records and the agencies responsible for them
- determine which records can be released to the public after a prescribed number of years
- confirm which records should be kept and which should be destroyed
- determine where, how and by whom records no longer required at the agency premises should be stored or destroyed.

Local Archives

Local archives can be at provincial, state or lower (e.g., municipal) governmental level. The principles that govern these collections are the same as those for other archival collections.

Storage is always a problem for archival collections. In addition, as the formats of documents change from paper to electronic, many fundamental principles must be re-examined.

EXERCISE 13.1

Find and list the names of any archival collections in your locality. Indicate the types of archive you have found (whether government, local, or private collection, etc.) and briefly describe each collection.

Information Agencies

Community Information Agencies

Community information agencies provide information to meet the everyday needs of people in the community. They deal with two levels of information:

- survival information
    - housing
    - income
    - health
    - law
    - human rights
    - employment
- local information
    - recreation
    - education
    - local events
    - community developments
    - tourism.

Types of Community Information Agencies

- Government-funded community information agencies provide:
    - social welfare information
    - career reference centers
    - government shopfronts
    - tourist bureaus.

- Agencies which receive some government funding include:
    - citizens' advice bureaus (CAB)
    - community information and referral services
    - resource directories.

- Voluntary agencies offer telephone services, and facilities for special interest groups – e.g., women, victims of crime, ethnic groups, refugees.

Characteristics of Community Information Agencies

Community agencies may have the following features:

- some degree of reliance on volunteers to perform an advisory role
- training for volunteers, usually given by supervising professionals
- very small budgets
- lack of formal networking (although these services are aware of other agencies and refer clients to them).

Public Library or Community Information Agency?

Libraries may often appear to be in competition with community information agencies, but the focus of each of these information services varies, as highlighted below.

Public Library

Public libraries rely on material that is produced by others and is chosen to meet the needs of the clients. The information has been chosen impartially for its completeness, accuracy and balance. A person asking for information will be given the facts, not an interpretation of the facts or advice. Library staff need to be aware of other information agencies, use their published material and, when appropriate, refer users to the appropriate agency.

Community Information Agency

In community information agencies, clients are often given advice, interpretation and/or counselling in addition to information. The information provider may be committed to the interests of the client—e.g., the tenants' advice service. Verbal information is important. Material may be produced inhouse by the agency, and is often given away.

Commercial Information Agencies

Some private agencies operate information services for profit. These usually serve the business community. Clients often do not have the time, resources or expertise to do the research themselves but are willing to pay for a confidential information service.

Other Information Agencies

There are other information agencies that often perform a multitude of functions, e.g., as an archive, a library, an information agency, a war or battle memorial or historic site. Other organizations that provide information in a variety of formats include museums, art galleries, local history displays.

150   LEARN ABOUT INFORMATION

Exercise 13.2

Find one information agency in each of these categories in your community, then answer the following questions.

	Library	Archive	Records Management Unit	Community Information Agency
What type of information is collected?				
How is the information arranged?				
How do users find the information they require?				
Can users retrieve the information themselves?				
Who are the users?				
Can the users borrow the material?				
Who looks after the material?				

CHAPTER FOURTEEN
Client-Centered Information

Introduction
All information agencies are client-based organizations. To justify their continued existence, they must provide services that satisfy the information needs of their clients. This may lead to an increase in the client base, or increased demand for service. However, agencies must ascertain the needs of their clients before new programs and services are implemented.

Information agencies should be aware of how they can best serve their clients and what services could best meet their clients' needs. At times this may also require that they handle complaints, suggestions and criticism from their clients and have policies to handle each of these situations. Having effective policies in place and carrying them out should result in improved services.

Measuring Client Satisfaction
Information agencies need to determine the attitudes of their users and know whether they are satisfied with the information and the service provided. It is important to determine whether clients are satisfied with the services provided.

Many information agencies conduct regular surveys of users, or rely on basic statistics such as the number of loans and people through the door. Information agencies should also be interested in why people do not use their services, and need to look for ways to capture this information.

Surveys
An effective way to find out how an information agency's community feels about the services provided is to conduct a survey.

User Surveys
Surveys in information agencies typically examine levels of satisfaction with a range of services such as opening hours, types of materials selected, users' awareness of the services, or the outcomes of the services provided. Information agencies need to be alert to the 'halo' effect, where users give positive answers to please the questioner. To neutralize this effect patrons are able to complete surveys online, using one of the online survey creators available, such as Survey Monkey (http://www.surveymonkey.com/), Google Forms (http://www.google.com.au/forms), or SurveyGizmo (http://www.surveygizmo.com), so that users can maintain their anonymity. Person-to-person surveys conducted by people other than library staff also allow users to express their views more freely.

User and Non-User Surveys
This type of survey asks non-users why they do not use a particular information agency. Once the responses have been collated and considered, identified problems can be addressed

using solutions like publicity drives and increased services. The survey may find that potential clients are using other information agencies to satisfy their needs.

A Case Study

A particular library service covers a large area, but has the lowest usage of any library service in the state. The library management wished to obtain information from the general community to try to increase the use of the library service so decided to survey non-users of the library.

The survey aimed to :
- establish a profile of non-users according to age, gender, work status, residential details, past and potential use of the library, and attitude towards a library service.
- find out reasons for non-use
- measure knowledge of available services and obtain opinions on other services that should be offered.

A non-user was defined as someone who had not used the library in the last twelve months. This included use of the photocopier, making a telephone enquiry, or attending any sessions offered by the library, in addition to traditional library services such as reference use and borrowing.

Only people over eighteen years of age were surveyed because the local schools actively encouraged children to use the library regularly.

Volunteers, rather than library staff, conducted the survey. Survey forms were distributed and collected by the Friends of the Library group. Each volunteer had to locate five people who had not used the library in the previous twelve months. 150 forms were given out and 137 were returned (providing a response rate of 91%).

The survey reinforced the library service's perceptions about why people did not use the library. The main reasons cited were 'not enough time to read', 'don't like reading', 'I get books elsewhere' and, significantly, 'unsure of the services available'.

The library service used this survey in their future planning to promote the service more generally within the community, and to introduce more technology-based services.

Interestingly, the survey produced some unexpected byproducts. One was the enthusiastic involvement of the Friends of the Library that the library service hopes to cultivate and use. Another was that the publicity generated among non-users led to some of them becoming users of the library.

Number of Loans
In libraries, use can be measured by the number of loan transactions. This is often a reliable method of ascertaining library usage, and many libraries use this method to determine staffing levels, hours of opening and book selection. Basically, material is counted as it is

returned to the library. These statistics can be divided into subject areas, formats and reading levels to determine reader profiles and preferences.

However, this method does not take account of the clients who use the library for non-borrowing purposes such as viewing DVDs in the library, photocopying, consulting the reference collection, using electronic resources, browsing through periodicals and attending special programs. Numbers can be counted for other services such as reference questions received. It is not possible to gauge whether users are satisfied with particular aspects of the service, nor why non-users do not use the service when assessing the library only on the basis of the number of loans.

Number of Users
This method counts people as they enter the information agency—the 'turnstile' method. It is a quantitative measure, not a qualitative one, as the information agency has no knowledge of how these people use their services, once they enter. Is the information agency being visited as an information resource or just because it's a warm refuge on a cold day?

Exercise 14.1

List ways a library in your area, the library you use most regularly, or the library where you work, could measure client satisfaction.

Communication with Clients

Being able to communicate effectively is a basic requirement of working in any information agency. Every aspect of the work—from identifying a client's need to locating information and handling complaints—requires good communication skills.

In particular, staff need to be able to:
- make clients feel welcome
- smile often as this puts people at ease
- find out what information the client needs to know (this often requires clarification by staff)
- help clients find information for themselves
- refer clients to other sources of information
- inform clients of the regulations of the information agency
- communicate easily with colleagues.

Good client service means developing a relationship with clients that encourages them to use the service and feel confident in asking for help. Good client service also allows clients the freedom to comment on the service provided.

Every service organization has policies and procedures for dealing with clients. These provide the foundation for staff behavior and relationships with clients. It is essential that all staff familiarize themselves with policies and procedures, as it will give all staff consistent understanding of the practices and procedures of the information agency and confidence in dealing with clients.

Communication Channels

Traditionally, library staff and their users communicated in a face-to-face environment but over the years technology has introduced a vast array of options into the information agency world. Most information agencies allow their clients to phone, email, send instant messages, engage in chat room exchanges, SMS, Skype, send Facebook and Twitter messages and use many of the other social media channels available. Some of these media allow one-on-one exchanges while the purposes of others are to provide one-to-many broadcasts.

Information agencies need to consider whether and how different communication channels impact on:
- volume of queries (i.e., its acceptance by users)
- types of queries
- expected response times
- ease of conducting reference interviews.

Information agencies should consider other aspects of communication between users and the agency, such as:
- which communication channels will be most suited to the agency's environment
- the impact of starting a new communication channel when others are already available
- why users choose one communication channel over others.

CHAPTER FOURTEEN   Client-Centered Information   155

Regardless of the communication options available for use by both information agency staff and clients, it is important that a centralized strategy be adopted when deciding which communication channels are made available. It is also important to decide which staff will monitor and reply to messages and in what environment they will do so.

EXERCISE 14.2

Look at the communication options available in a library in your area, the library you use most regularly, or the library where you work.

1. What communication channels are available in the library?

2. Are different communication options encouraged?

3. How do you communicate with the library staff? Why do you use this method?

4. Would other communication options engage users more effectively?

Handling Complaints

Most complaints can be dealt with using good communication skills. Clients usually want to be listened to, taken seriously and treated with respect. You may be able to explain why a policy exists, or how it is applied. If the client is dissatisfied, he or she will need to be referred to a more senior staff person.

An apology for a perceived mistake is often the quickest way to resolve a complaint.

All complaints, suggestions and comments must be treated seriously. Therefore, many libraries have forms for clients to complete when they make a complaint, either on paper or online. These forms should be examined by management to determine the cause of the complaint. When necessary, management should instigate measures to rectify the situation.

A good complaint handling system is built on:

- **Culture**: libraries must value complaints as a means of improving their relations with the public.

- **Principles**: an effective complaint handling system must be modelled on the principles of fairness, accessibility, responsiveness, efficiency and integration.

- **People**: staff who deal with complaints must be skilled and professional.

- **Process**: the seven stages of complaint handling—acknowledgment, assessment, planning, investigation, response, review, and consideration of systemic issues—should be clearly outlined.
    1. A complaint should be acknowledged promptly.
    2. The complaint should be assessed and assigned priority.
    3. If investigation is required, it should be planned.
    4. The investigation should resolve factual issues and consider options for complaint.
    5. The response to the complainant should be clear, informative and timely
    6. If the complainant is not satisfied with the response, internal review of the decision should be offered and information about external review options should be provided. The complainant should be kept informed of how the matter is being considered and ultimately addressed.
    7. Any systemic issues that arise as a result of the complaint should be considered and acted on.

- **Analysis**: information about complaints should be examined as part of a continuous process of organizational review and improvement.

Doing the job right   +   Effective customer contact   =   Increased customer satisfaction
   the first time   /complaint handling   /support

Effectively handling a complaint can have the following twofold effect.
- It can help resolve dissatisfaction about the service that a person did or did not receive.
- The complaint can assist management to identify problems and change procedures to prevent similar dissatisfactions and complaints in future.

ACTIVITY 14.3

If possible, participate in a role-playing exercise with others, taking turns to be an unhappy library client and a staff member.

Debrief the role-play. Ask participants what behaviors they observed, whether or not the staff member followed appropriate steps and what you think the outcome will be.

If you are not able to participate in a role play, list the appropriate steps to follow in dealing with a complaint in the library.

In summary, to ensure quality service and user satisfaction, information providers need to:
- establish direct channels of communication with current and potential user groups
- continually evaluate trends in information needs by surveying users
- evaluate measures of information services, such as surveys, particularly to provide facts for bargaining with funding bodies
- establish and maintain liaison with administrators
- give presentations on new information resources as they become available
- provide regular user education seminars
- use a range of communication channels, including social media, to provide a higher profile.

CHAPTER FIFTEEN
Information Standards and Ethics

Introduction
It is essential that all staff working in information agencies have a level of understanding of the standards, ethics and legislation appropriate to the information environment. Records and information management standards based on nationally and internationally accepted best practice can assist agencies to comply with legislation and ensure effective management of their records. This chapter considers some of the relevant aspects of standards, ethics and legislation.

Standards
Standards are the criteria by which services and programs are measured or assessed. Established by professional organizations, accrediting bodies or government agencies, the criteria may set out the minimum requirements needed to ensure that a product, material or procedure will do what it is intended to do.

In the community, standards are developed by standards associations at national and international levels, and are applied to many products and procedures. The standards are arrived at after consultation with industry and union representatives, government officials and members of the community. Standards are not legally binding although some have been incorporated into legislation. Citizens expect that standards indicate a level of excellence and a mark of acceptance.

Types of Standards
- Standards may be standards of adequacy or standards of excellence.
- Procedural standards are written instructions that detail how a specific function is to be undertaken.
- Competency standards identify how tasks are to be performed and whether someone is working proficiently in their job.
- Quantitative standards are a precise measurement, simple to apply, and may cover staff, space, budget etc.
- Qualitative standards evaluate such factors as staffing characteristics and complexity of material and are more difficult to apply.
- Minimum standards set preliminary goals for new or developing institutions or services.
- Informal standards are often the product of accumulated experience.

Standards can be both quantitative and qualitative in respect to buildings, materials, staff, services and collections. They may be standards of excellence giving measures to which the services of information agencies can aspire, or minimum levels that indicate basic requirements. Standards documents set criteria for the decisions and actions of those concerned with the planning, administration and accreditation of services. They deal with matters of service or performance, as well as procedural, educational and technical issues. They also present goals towards which the profession can aspire. Procedural standards and guidelines describe an acceptable or agreed-upon method of accomplishing a particular type of library activity or task. Examples are the cataloging guidelines, *Resource description and access*, and standards for interlibrary loans, *Guidelines for best practice in interlibrary loan and document delivery*.

International standards
International standards allow organizations across the world to interact with each other and maintain consistency in their approach to products, services and systems. This ensures quality, safety and efficiency.

The International Organization for Standardization (ISO) describes a standard as "a document that provides requirements, specifications, guidelines or characteristics that can be used consistently to ensure that materials, products, processes and services are fit for their purpose".

Among the information environments, many international standards have been developed and adopted. Some of them are briefly outlined below.
- **Libraries**: The International Federation of Library Associations and Institutions (IFLA) and many national library associations have developed cataloging tools for libraries to use when they are preparing their standards. Some of the following international standards have been adopted in many libraries.
    - RDA (Resource Description and Access) provides the cataloger with instructions and guidelines for recording bibliographic data. RDA uses key bibliographic elements of interest to users (e.g., title, statement of responsibility, physical details) and emphasizes their relationships. It deals with what to record, not how to record it.
    - International Standard Bibliographic Description (ISBD) provides a framework for creating bibliographic descriptions in a consistent, human-readable form. It lists all elements required to describe and identify all types of material; assigns an order to the elements; and prescribes punctuation to precede each element.
    - MARC (MAchine Readable Cataloging) records describe resources in a consistent way by labeling each piece of bibliographic information, so that automated systems can read and manipulate it. MARC was developed to allow libraries to share cataloging by providing a format that can be read and understood by different library information systems.
- **Archives**: Since it has only been in recent times that archives have begun to share their records and data, there are fewer established standards to describe their collections. Here are a number of those adopted at the international level.
    - General International Standard Archival Description (ISAD(G)) defines the elements that should be included in an archival finding aid. ISAD(G) contains a list of elements and rules to describe archives and the information that should be included in descriptions.
    - Encoded Archival Description (EAD) is a data standard for describing archives. EAD enables archives, museums, libraries, and manuscript repositories to create finding aids that are easy to search, maintain and exchange.

- **Museums**: Most resources found in museum collections are unique to that institution. The digital age has encouraged museums to share their collections with a wider audience. This has highlighted the need to develop for standard ways of recording data about the resources held.
  - The International Committee for Documentation (CIDOC), a committee of the International Council of Museums (ICOM) created International guidelines for museum object information: the CIDOC information categories to standardize the way that museum objects are described.
- **Other information agencies**: It is difficult to identify international standards for other information agencies as they cover such a wide range of subjects and types of resources. Specific information agencies may use community standards and best practices to establish quality baselines, facilitate cooperation among and between information agencies and other organizations, and enable the exchange of data between systems.

Professional Statements

Allied to standards are professional statements issued by industry and professional organizations detailing decisions about procedures and ethical practices that are acceptable to members. Information agencies sometimes issue statements that reflect their members' philosophical, ethical and professional ideals. Examples include statements on:

- free information service for all
- professional appointments
- literacy
- services to minority groups.

EXERCISE 15.1

Locate the home page for the national library association in your country and find a professional statement that relates to a library you use or work in.
How would this statement affect the services of this library?

Ethics

Introduction

Information agencies deal with a commodity—information—that is in great demand and can be used in a variety of ways. The relationship between the agency, the client and the information has many ethical, legal, moral and procedural implications. Statements of ethics, codes of behavior and laws governing privacy and protecting intellectual property have been devised to facilitate correct procedures in dealing with information.

As representatives of members of the information industry, professional associations are usually the bodies that draft, implement and monitor ethical standards within the profession. Some professional bodies hold disciplinary hearings to judge breaches of these standards, imposing fines and withdrawing accreditation.

In the information industry ethical decisions need to be made on such issues as:
- censorship
- confidentiality of clients' records
- free service or user-pays
- freedom of access to information
- sponsorship
- fairness and equity in service
- equality in employment.

Statements on Professional Ethics

Librarians all over the world are well aware of their profession's ethical implications. In more than sixty countries library associations have developed and approved a national code of ethics for librarians. These codes can be accessed at http://www.ifla.org/faife/professional-codes-of-ethics-for-librarians. The *IFLA code of ethics for librarians and other information workers* was endorsed in August 2012.

The Australian statement of professional conduct located at http://www.alia.org.au/about-alia/policies-standards-and-guidelines/statement-professional-conduct reinforces the ethical commitment of those in the profession "to ensure the free flow of information and ideas", and to recognize that "the interactions between library and information services and their clients should be guided by the highest standards of service quality and characterized by the highest levels of integrity". The statement details ethical standards for providing services, and for ensuring intellectual freedom. It recognizes the rights of intellectual property owners, and the privacy of clients. It also warns against situations where personal interests and philosophies may differ from those of the employing institution or the profession.

The Chartered Institute of Library and Information Professionals (CILIP) in the UK has a code of professional practice accessible at http://www.cilip.org.uk/cilip/about/ethics/code-professional-practice). It:
- stresses that members of the Institute must not engage in professional misconduct within the field of librarianship and information services
- spells out what constitutes misconduct (e.g., discrimination, privacy, refusing to supply information or knowingly supplying misleading information)
- briefly refers to the likely consequences.

The Code of Ethics of the American Library Association was adopted as ALA Policy 54.16 (http://www.ala.org/advocacy/proethics/codeofethics/codeethics). It states:

> "As members of the American Library Association, we recognize the importance of codifying and making known to the profession and to the general public the ethical principles that guide the work of librarians, other professionals providing information services, library trustees and library staffs.
>
> Ethical dilemmas occur when values are in conflict. The American Library Association Code of Ethics states the values to which we are committed, and embodies the ethical responsibilities of the profession in this changing information environment."

Ethical Qualities
Library staff should:
- aim to provide a high level of service
- ensure equity of service where all user groups are treated equally, recognizing and accounting for the differing information and access needs of different users
- provide a balanced collection which presents all aspects of subjects. The issue of censorship is problematic for many libraries as they strive to present material of literary merit, balanced intellectual content and contemporary commentary.

ACTIVITY 15.2

Look at the following ethical situations that may arise in a library. How would you deal with them? You may wish to discuss them with fellow students or colleagues.

1. A neighbour, whom you have been fighting for years about his barking dog, asks you for some information on the Noise Control legislation.

2. A library user comes to the desk to tell you that another user is searching for pornographic material on the Internet and asks you to tell the person to stop.

3. In a joint-use library, who has priority for service? If a parent wants to borrow on behalf of his student child, should the parent take precedence over another student?

4. A library user continues to talk loudly on their mobile phone in the library's study area. Should mobile phones be banned from libraries?

5. A professor at your university demands the removal of a rival professor's publications on the grounds that they are incorrect.

6. A library patron has complained that the library holds a copy of Hitler's *Mein Kampf*. Should a library contain material advocating particular points of view?

Legislation that Impacts on Provision of Information

In most countries legislation has been enacted that impacts on how and when information may be provided. This section provides a broad overview on the legal implications of:
- copyright
- privacy acts
- freedom of information
- public lending right.

Copyright

Copyright protects created works so that the creators can enjoy the fruits of their labors. Works covered include written material, artistic and musical works, compilations, computer programs, films, sound recordings and broadcasts. The copyright of a work is separate from the work itself. It can be bought and sold as a separate, valuable entity.

The owner of copyright may vary from the creator to the place of employment of the creator if the work was created in the course of their work. This also includes commissioned material and work published in a newspaper or journal.

Copyright of works produced after 1977 in the United States lasts for 70 years after the death of the creator but only 50 years in Canada. Most international works are also covered by the federal Copyright Act of 1976 in the United States. Australia's copyright legislation underwent changes in 2004 to bring it into line with the USA and the European Union—copyright now lasts for 70 years after the creator's death. However, as this change was not made retrospective, anything created prior to 2004 is still subject to a 50 year ruling.

Infringement of copyright—that is, using the work without the copyright owner's permission—can have legal consequences. Special provisions in the copyright law exempt certain uses of material, for example, information agencies such as libraries may copy material without permission under strict guidelines. These include displaying the copyright provisions near the photocopier and signing photocopying declaration forms for interlibrary loans.

Some institutions, such as school authorities and tertiary institutions, pay fees to allow them to copy and record material for their students' use.

Libraries need to be aware of their responsibilities with copyright legislation in their country.

EXERCISE 15.3

Locate a copy of the copyright legislation that is used in your country or state.

1. What is the name of the copyright legislation used in your country or state?

2. Are there amendments which also need to be taken into account?

3. Have specific copyright arrangements been established for libraries and other cultural institutions? If so, what are they?

Privacy Acts

Privacy laws deal with the regulation of personal information about individuals which can be collected by governments, public, and private organizations and its storage and use. Privacy laws protect the privacy rights of an individual or their reasonable expectation of privacy.

In the United States, legislation affecting the privacy or confidentiality of library records has been enacted by most states, but not by the federal government. The thrust of these acts is to protect the rights of individuals by ensuring that unauthorized persons are denied access to information about what library materials are being used by whom, and by requiring that law enforcement agencies follow strict procedures before being given access to this information. However, the USA Patriot Act of 2001 overrides all such state laws by giving federal law enforcement agencies power to examine library records, records of bookstore purchases, the contents of computer drives and other personal records, in order to gather information about possible criminal terrorist activity. In addition, libraries and other agencies are forbidden from making public the fact that they are subject to such investigation.

Privacy in Canada is governed by the Privacy Act of 1985. Its purpose is to "extend the present laws of Canada that protect the privacy of individuals with respect to personal information about themselves held by a government institution ...". The Privacy Act also extends the present laws of Canada "that provide individuals with a right of access to that information." It should be noted that this law applies specifically to personal information kept by government agencies, and not to businesses or corporations.

Australia's Privacy Act 1988 details the Australian Government's commitment to the privacy of individuals' personal details held by government departments and agencies. It is also a useful guide for other organizations in handling confidential client records. It ensures the protection of personal information in the possession of federal government departments and agencies and safeguards for the collection and use of tax file numbers. The Privacy Amendment (Private Sector) Act 2000 extended coverage of the Act to most private sector organizations.

In the United Kingdom there is no independent tort law that recognizes the right to privacy. However, as a member of the European Convention on Human Rights, the UK adheres to Article 8 ECHR, that guarantees 'everyone has the right to respect for his private and family life'.

Libraries should be aware of these laws and principles as they handle confidential private records of clients.

Freedom of Information (FOI)
Freedom of Information legislation gives people a legal right to see documents concerning themselves that are held by government departments and agencies. The governments of individual countries, states and territories have their own Freedom of Information legislation. The implications for libraries and archives include requests made to access restricted material, and access to decisions about materials, services and users. Library and archive staff need to be able to direct users to the provisions of the legislation for their information needs.

Public Lending Right
Public Lending Right (PLR) is a compensation program. PLR makes payments to eligible creators and publishers on the basis that income is lost from the availability of their books in public lending libraries. Payment is determined by the number of copies of eligible books that are held in public lending libraries. This information is obtained from an annual survey of the books held in a sample of public lending libraries. Selected libraries are required to check the lending records of certain books. For example, in Australia if fifty or more copies of an eligible book are estimated to be held in Australian public lending libraries a payment may be made.

Twenty-eight countries have a PLR program and others are considering adopting one. Canada, the United Kingdom, all the Scandinavian countries, Germany, Austria, Belgium, the Netherlands, Israel, Australia, and New Zealand all currently have a PLR program. There is ongoing debate in France about implementing one. There is also a move towards having a Europe-wide PLR program administered by the European Union.

PLR programs vary from country to country. Some, like Germany and the Netherlands, have linked PLR to copyright legislation and have made libraries liable to pay authors for every book in their collection. Other countries do not connect PLR to copyright. For countries such as Canada or Australia the majority of funds would be going to authors outside the country, mostly in the United States. This would not be acceptable in those countries.

In Denmark, this program is not considered as reimbursement of potential lost sales, rather it is government support of the arts. Works that are supported include: books, music, and visual artworks that have been created and published in Denmark, and available in public and school libraries.

The way that payments are determined also varies from country to country. Some countries pay according to the number of times a book has been taken out of a library, others use a system of payment based on whether a library owns a book. The amount paid is minimal and varies from country to country.

Different countries also have differing eligibility criteria. In most nations only published works are accepted and government publications, bibliographies and dictionaries are rarely counted. Some PLR services are mandated solely to fund literary works of fiction, and some countries, such as Norway, have a sliding scale paying far less to non-fiction works. Many nations also exclude scholarly and academic texts.

ACTIVITY 15.4

Identify the legislation that impacts on the provision of information in your country or state. Make sure that you include: copyright, privacy and freedom of information legislation.
Familiarize yourself with this legislation and its requirements for you.

ANSWERS

Some of the suggested answers are, by the nature of the questions, only a guide. Use these answers to stimulate your own thoughts if you have difficulty with an exercise.

Answers are not included where each response is likely to be different (e.g., personal response, individual examples).

EXERCISE 1.3

You may need to discuss these answers as some sources of information can be considered both primary and secondary (e.g., the reporting in a newspaper (primary) which also includes comments (secondary) about the information).

	Primary Source	**Secondary Source**	**Tertiary Source**
1	Yes		
2	Yes		
3	Yes		
4	Yes		
5	Yes		
6	Yes		
7		Yes	
8		Yes	
9		Yes	
10		Yes	
11			Yes
12			Yes
13			Yes

REVISION QUIZ 1.4

1. Apart from text, what other methods are used to present information?
   Information can be presented as data, images, text, documents and sound.

2. What are the five characteristics of good information highlighted in this chapter?
   Information must be: relevant; timely; accurate and complete; concise; and unambiguous.

3. What makes information useful for decision-making?
   For information to be useful for decision-making, it must be: the right information; available at the right time; available to the right person; at the right cost; in the right format to facilitate a decision.

4. Name three sources of information. What distinguishes them from each other?
   Three sources of information are primary, secondary and tertiary.

Primary sources provide first-hand information or direct evidence of a time and place. They are original documents that contain first-hand information.

Secondary sources are interpretations based on the examination of primary sources. They provide comments on events, discoveries etc.

Tertiary sources present summaries, condensed versions or overviews of materials, and usually refer back to primary or secondary sources. They often provide information in a context to assist in interpreting it.

Exercise 3.1

1. What is the meaning of the word shindy?
   Dictionary – in print or online

2. I need a recipe for spaghetti bolognaise.
   Recipe book, website, ask a friend, magazine

3. What is the quickest route to drive from London to Liverpool?
   Road map, motoring association, Google maps (or similar website), GPS system

4. My toilet is leaking. Where can I find the name of a plumber?
   Yellow Pages, ask a friend, trade directory, online

5. Who wrote the book *The shipping news*?
   Bibliography, library catalog, online search, phone a bookshop

6. If I am fined for speeding, how much will I have to pay?
   Contact police station, ask a friend, government information service or shopfront, local government website

7. I need the address of Kwik-Kopy Printing Centre in Toronto.
   Phone book, trade directory, website

8. How would I obtain legal advice about a dispute with my neighbour?
   Citizens' Advice Bureaus, Legal Aid Office

9. My child has swallowed snail bait. What should I do?
   First Aid manual, phone Poisons Information, contact hospital, doctor, health clinic

10. Which bank will give me the best interest rate on a long-term deposit?
    Contact banks, newspaper article, ask friends, bank websites

11. Who was Louis Pasteur?
    Encyclopedia, biographical dictionary, Internet

12. My child is writing a report on snakes. Where can I find some information?
    Encyclopedia, public library, Internet, brochures from the zoo

Exercise 3.2

You could include the following:

Planning a Holiday	For Employment	Applying for Study
go to tourist bureau for brochures	*read newspaper*	*check online for suitable courses*
search online sites	*view online sites*	*read course details*
look at transport timetables	*write résumé or CV*	*attend information sessions*
read accommodation guides	*write letters of applications*	*talk to academic staff*
check weather forecasts!	*obtain references*	*fill in application*
	copy qualifications	*reply to letter of offer*

Exercise 3.4

All of these sources of information are likely to contain some information of interest, but you should have thought of the following points:

1. An article titled 'System identification and model-predictive control of office buildings with integrated photovoltaic-thermal collectors, radiant floor heating and active thermal storage' from *Solar Energy*, volume 113, March 2015, Pages 139–157.
   This article is likely to be authoritative but is fairly technical so would only be useful if a technical report is required.

2. A monograph titled *Fundamentals of solar heating*, written by Richard Schubert and L.D. Ryan that was published by Prentice-Hall in 1981.
   This article was authoritative in its time but is far too old to be useful now. It would be worth checking which other sources have cited it to look at more recent information.

3. An editorial from *The guardian* of July 7 2014 titled 'Solar has won. Even if coal were free to burn, power stations couldn't compete'.
   This editorial would contain the most recent information and may help provide ideas for discussion but would not give much detail.

4. Wikipedia article titled *Solar power*, last modified on December 12 2014.
   This article would be useful during the early stages of research as it would provide general background information when you define and characterize the scope of the report. It may include a bibliography or suggested reading.

5. A pamphlet called *Get your power from the sun* published by the US Department of Energy, Office of Energy Efficiency and Renewable Energy in 2003.
   This pamphlet is not likely to be useful, even though it is from an authoritative source, because it is too out-of-date.

6. An article 'Potential for concentrating solar power to provide baseload and dispatchable power' published in *Nature climate change*, volume 4, June 2014, pages 689–692.
   This article may provide useful information.

7. A Web article written for children, posted in 2010, titled *How do solar panels work*.

This web article was written for children so would give a simple explanation. It may not be useful but could provide some background understanding. The author may not be considered to be an authority on the subject.

8. A monograph written by Sandra Bright titled *Examining solar energy,* published in 2013. *This monograph is likely to be a useful source, but remember the time lapse between the preparation of the information and its publication. It may contain a bibliography which would lead to other sources.*

EXERCISE 4.1

archival materials – *print or electronic*	microforms – *non-print*
blogs – *electronic*	models – *non-print*
books/monographs – *print*	newspapers – *print or electronic*
brochures – *print*	oral history recordings – *non-print or electronic*
business records – *print or electronic*	pamphlets – *print*
catalogs – *print or non-print or electronic*	patents – *print or electronic*
CD-ROMs – *non-print*	personal documents – *print or electronic*
conference proceedings – *print or electronic*	photographs – *non-print*
DVDs – *non-print*	pictures – *non-print*
e-journals – *electronic*	posters – *non-print*
electronic databases – *electronic*	radio programs – *non-print*
ephemera – *print*	RSS feeds – *electronic*
files/transactions – *print or electronic*	serials/journals/periodicals/magazines – *print or electronic*
films – *non-print*	slides – *non-print*
government publications – *print or electronic*	streaming video – *electronic*
gramophone records – *non-print*	technical drawings – *non-print*
grey literature – *print or electronic*	theses – *print or electronic*
indexes – *print or electronic*	TV programs – *non-print*
kits – *non-print & electronic*	USB drives – *electronic*
letters – *print or electronic*	videocassettes – *non-print*
maps – *non-print or electronic*	websites – *electronic*

EXERCISE 4.3

Term	Definition	Type
Appendix	*Additional material such as statistics, tables etc., attached as a separate item at the end of a resource*	*Print or Electronic*
Banner	*1. The strip of information on the front page of a newspaper that contains editorial and publishing details. 2. A narrow strip of advertising or identification of ownership on a web page*	*Print or Electronic*

Bi-annual	*Issued twice a year*	*Print or Electronic*
Bibliography	*A list of materials or resources, usually either subject-related or on the works of one author*	*Print or Electronic*
Biennial	*Issued every two years*	*Print or Electronic*
Caption	*A heading at the beginning of text or a chapter, section etc.*	*Print or Electronic*
Cartographic	*Representing the whole or part of the earth or any celestial body (e.g. a map)*	*Non-print or Electronic*
CIP	*Cataloging-in-publication. Cataloging data produced by the national library or other agency of the country of publication, included in the work when it is published*	*Print or Electronic*
Contents page	*The page at the front of a book or serial which lists the contents in the order in which they appear*	*Print or Electronic*
Copyright	*The right given by law to authors, composers and publishers to sell, reproduce or publish a resource during a stated given time*	*Print or Electronic*
Dedication	*The author's inscription to a particular person or persons*	*Print or Electronic*
Dimensions	*1. Size. 2. In RDA, the measurement of the carrier and/or the container of a resource*	*Print or Non-Print*
Discography	*A bibliography of sound recordings (gramophone records, audiocassettes, compact discs), often by one artist, group etc.*	*Print or Electronic*
DOI	*Digital Object Identifier. An identification system for intellectual property in the digital environment that aims to provide a framework for managing intellectual content, linking customers with publishers, facilitating electronic commerce, and enabling automated copyright management. DOIs are persistent identifiers for electronic documents, articles and other resources*	*Electronic*
Duration	*Length of time e.g., for a film, or playing time for a CD-ROM etc.*	*Non-Print*
Dust jacket	*Paper cover for a hard bound book*	*Print*
Edition	*All the copies of a work produced from the original source*	*Print or Electronic*
Frequency:	*Interval between issues of a serial (e.g., weekly, quarterly)*	*Print or Electronic*
Glossary	*An alphabetical list of definitions*	*Print or Electronic*
Half-title	*The brief title of a book which appears on the leaf preceding the title page*	*Print or Electronic*

Hardware	1. Audiovisual equipment (e.g., slide projector, 16 mm projector etc.). 2. Computer equipment (e.g., computer, monitor, keyboard etc.)	Non-Print or Electronic
Holdings	Stock of a library or information centre	Print or Non-Print or Electronic
Illustrations	Pictures, photographs or other visual matter that clarify, decorate or embellish a text	Non-Print
Impression	All copies of an edition of a work printed at one time	Print
Imprint	Publication details - place, publisher, date of publication	Print or Electronic
Index	1. An alphabetical list of terms or topics in a book, usually found at the back. 2. A systematically arranged list that indicates the contents of a document or group of documents	Print or Electronic
Introduction	A preliminary statement to a work outlining the scope of the following text, and often written by an accepted authority in the subject area	Print or Electronic
ISBN	International Standard Book Number. A number intended to be unique, assigned by an agency in each country to all resources published. Identifies the publisher, language and title	Print or Electronic
ISSN	International Standard Serial Number. An internationally recognized number assigned to each serial publication	Print or Electronic
Preface	The author's or editor's reasons for the book. It appears after the title page and before the introduction	Print or Electronic
Quarterly	A publication issued at three monthly intervals, four times a year	Print or Electronic
Reprint	A new printing of a work made from the original type face	Print
Software	1. Audiovisual material (e.g., slides, 16mm motion picture etc.) 2. Computer program(s), that tells the computer what to do	Non-Print or Electronic
Spine	The part of a book's cover which holds the front and back together	Print
Title page	The page in a printed resource that provides the most complete information about the author and title, and is used as a primary source of cataloging data	Print
Verso	The back of a leaf of a book (e.g., verso of the title page)	Print or Electronic

ANSWERS 175

EXERCISE 5.3

1. How to fill in tax forms.
   Internet

2. Article from a peer-reviewed journal.
   Databases

3. A specific website
   Internet

4. Information on a new topic
   More likely Internet as it won't have been written about in published documents.

5. Biographical information
   Both Internet and Databases

6. Statistical information
   Both Internet and Databases

REVISION QUIZ 5.4

1. Define online portals.
   An online portal is an entry point to the Internet that provides access to electronic information including websites, ftp sites, databases and indexes to print resources in a subject area such as agriculture

2. What similarities are there between discovery layers and federated searches?
   Discovery layers and federated searches:
   - *are the starting point for research when the research needs are broad*
   - *search and provide direct access to individual journal articles*
   - *have customized content, as their tools default to searching resources owned by or accessible through the individual library*
   - *include most journals in the library's collections*
   - *offer basic as well as advanced searching*
   - *indicate the database that articles come from*
   - *offer additional features such as formatting and importing citations, and tagging*
   - *have open source as well as commercial options.*

3. Explain the differences between keyword searches and subject searches.
   Keyword searches use natural language. It is necessary to decide what are the important words or phrases relevant to the topic. Then, type these keywords into the search box.

   Subject searching involves searching the subject headings that have been assigned to each item in a database. By searching these headings you are able to find relevant items on the same topic. To find subject headings for a topic, see if the database has an online or published thesaurus to browse for subjects that match the topic. This information is usually available on the Help screens.

4. What are five advanced search features you could use when searching in databases?

Any of these would be appropriate answers.

- *Boolean Operators: are connecting words placed between search terms to narrow or expand a search.*

    AND: Helps to Narrow a Search = It tells the computer that both terms must be present in the record (e.g., fruit AND vegetables)

    OR: Helps to Broaden a Search = It is used for like or synonymous terms. Using it tells the computer that either term must be present in the record (e.g., fruit OR vegetables)

    NOT: Helps to Narrow a Search = It eliminates an unwanted search term or group of search terms from the search results (e.g., fruit NOT vegetables)

- *Truncation: broadens your search to take into account plurals, various word endings and spellings. To use truncation, enter the root of a word and put the truncation symbol at the end. The database will return results that include any ending of that root word (e.g., child* = child, childs, children, childrens, childhood). Truncation symbols may vary by database but common symbols include: *, !, ?, or #.*

- *Wildcards: substitute a symbol for one letter of a word. This allows you to adjust for variations in spelling within a word (e.g., wom?n = woman, women or defen?e = defense, defence). Not all search systems allow wildcard searching but for those that do, '?' is the most common wildcard symbol.*

- *Phrase Searching: Most databases allow you to specify that adjacent words be searched as phrases. Using parentheses or quotes around search words is a common way to do phrase searching (e.g., "global financial crisis"), but not all databases or search engines use them.*

- *Proximity Operators: Many databases allow you to specify that the words you are searching are within a certain proximity of each other. They vary according to the database, but some common ones include:*

    'w#' = with. Specifies that words appear in the order you type them in. Substitute the # with the number of words that may appear in between the words.

    'n#' = near. Specifies that the words may appear in any order. Substitute the # with a number of words that may appear in between the words.

- *Nesting: with a complicated search, you can put the various parts in parentheses, to make it easier for the computer to understand. This is useful when you are mixing ANDs and ORs (e.g., (fruit OR vegetables) AND (cereals OR grains)).*

- *Fields: contain specific pieces of bibliographic information in library databases. Common fields include: author, title, journal title, abstract, publisher, date of publication and subject. Limiting your search to specific fields can yield more precise results. To find various fields within a database, look for drop down boxes or menus to select the field you want to search. Then combine words and fields together with Boolean or proximity operators for a more precise search.*

- *Limiting: is another way to make your results more specific. Many of the same Field options (discussed above) are able to be used as limits; however, limit options will vary between databases.*
- *Searching for Information from a Specific Site: if you need information from a specific site, you can limit the search to a type of site (e.g., .edu or .gov) or to a specific domain (e.g., edu.ph). You do this by using the term 'site:' in the search (e.g., history AND site:edu.ph). A word of warning: this works in Google and some, but not all, other search engines.*

5. Name five ways that you could refine your search.
   Any of the following could be used
   To broaden your search, you should:
   - *check your spelling*
   - *consider using alternative keywords/subjects*
   - *use alternative spellings*
   - *use truncation symbols or wildcards to capture all forms of your keywords*
   - *check that you have used Boolean operators correctly*
   - *search other databases.*

   To narrow your search or make it more specific:
   - *add another concept and associated keywords*
   - *restrict your search to specific fields such as abstract*
   - *add search limiters to your search such as date range or peer-reviewed.*

EXERCISE 6.1

Social media sites you could have looked at and provided information on include, among others:

Academia.edu; About.me; Advogato; aNobii; AsianAvenue; aSmallWorld; Athlinks; Audimated.com; Bebo; Biip.no; BlackPlanet; Blauk; Blogster; Bolt.com; Busuu; Buzznet; CafeMom; Care2; CaringBridge; Classmates.com; Cloob; ClusterFlunk; CouchSurfing; CozyCot; Cross.tv; Crunchyroll; Cucumbertown; Cyworld; DailyBooth; DailyStrength; delicious; deviantART; Diaspora*; didlr; Disaboom; Dol2day; DontStayIn; Draugiem.lv; douban; DXY.cn; Elftown; Ello; Elixio; English, baby!; Epernicus; Eons.com; eToro; Experience Project; Exploroo; Faceparty; Faces.com; Fetlife; FilmAffinity; Filmow; FledgeWing; Flixster; Focus.com; Fotki; Fotolog; Foursquare; Friendica; Friends Reunited; Friendster; Frühstückstreff; Fuelmyblog; FullCircle; Gaia Online; GamerDNA; Gapyear.com; Gather.com; Gays.com; Geni.com; GetGlue; Gogoyoko; Goodreads; Goodwizz; Google+; GovLoop; Grono.net; Habbo; hi5; Hospitality Club; Hotlist; HR.com; Hub Culture; Hyves; Ibibo; Identi.ca; Indaba Music; Influenster; IRC-Galleria; Italki.com; Itsmy; iWiW; Jaiku; Jiepang; Kaixin001; Kiwibox; Lafango; LaiBhaari; Last.fm; LibraryThing; Lifeknot; LinkExpats; Listography; LiveJournal; Livemocha; Makeoutclub; MEETin; Meetup (website); Meettheboss; MillatFacebook; mixi; MocoSpace; MOG; MouthShut.com; Mubi; MyHeritage; MyLife; Myspace; Nasza-klasa.pl; Netlog; Nexopia; NGO Post; Ning; Odnoklassniki; Open Diary; OUTeverywhere; PatientsLikeMe; Partyflock; Pingsta; Plaxo; Playfire; Playlist.com; Plurk; Poolwo; Quechup; Qzone; Raptr; Ravelry; Renren; ReverbNation.com; Ryze; ScienceStage; Sgrouples; ShareTheMusic; Shelfari; Sina Weibo; Skoob; Skyrock; SocialVibe; Sonico.com; SoundCloud;

Spaces; Spot.IM; Spring.me; Stage 32; StudiVZ; Students Circle Network; StumbleUpon; Tagged; Talkbiznow; Taltopia; Taringa!; TeachStreet; TermWiki; The Sphere; TravBuddy.com; Travellerspoint; tribe.net; Trombi.com; Tuenti; Tylted; Vkontakte; Vampirefreaks.com; Viadeo; Virb; Vox; Wattpad; WAYN; WeeWorld; We Heart It; Wellwer; WeOurFamily; Wepolls.com; Wer-kennt-wen; weRead; Wiser.org; Wooxie; WriteAPrisoner.com; Xanga; XING; Xt3; Yammer; Yelp, Inc.; Yookos; Zoo.gr; Zooppa

(This is not an exhaustive list of social media sites.)

REVISION QUIZ 6.3

1. Define social media.
   Social media is a catch-all term used to describe a variety of Internet applications that allow users to create and share content, thus interacting with each other. This interaction can take many forms, but common types include:
   - *sharing links to interesting content produced by third parties*
   - *public updates to a profile, including information on current activities and even location data*
   - *sharing photos, videos and posts*
   - *commenting on photos, posts, updates, videos and links shared by others.*

2. What are the seven functions of social media outlined in this workbook?
   Social media can be grouped according to the functions performed by specific tools. They can be broken down into the following seven functional building blocks:
   identity; conversations; sharing; presence; relationships; reputation; groups.

3. What five steps could you take to use social media safely?
   Any of the following could be included:
   - *Ensure you have effective and updated antivirus/antispyware software and a firewall running before you go online.*
   - *Do not allow peer pressure to convince you to do something you are not comfortable with.*
   - *Be wary of publishing any identifying information about yourself—either in your profile or in your posts—such as phone numbers, pictures of your home, or your address.*
   - *Use a strong password that cannot easily be hacked.*
   - *Keep your profile closed and allow only your friends to view your profile.*
   - *Do not say anything or publish pictures that might later cause you or someone else embarrassment as once something is online it stays online.*
   - *Never post comments that may cause offense to any individual, group or organization.*
   - *Be aware of what friends post about you, or how they reply to your posts, particularly regarding your personal details and activities.*
   - *Be careful about what you say, what pictures you post, and how you present yourself in your profile, as many companies routinely view current or prospective employees' social media pages.*
   - *Use the privacy features of the social media site to restrict strangers' access to your profile, thus being guarded about who you let join your network.*

- *Be careful of phishing scams, including fake friend requests and posts from individuals or companies inviting you to visit other pages or sites.*
- *If you do get caught in a scam, make sure you remove any corresponding likes and permissions from your account.*

4. List three benefits of using social media.
   Some of the positive benefits of social media include: social participation; learning social skills; creating, managing and distributing content; exploring and learning; developing new skills.

EXERCISE 7.1

1. Who is the author?
   Helen Rowe – author. Front cover and title page

2. What is the title of the book?
   Learn about information. Front cover and title page

3. Is there a subtitle? What is it?
   No subtitle.

4. Where was the book published?
   Friendswood, Texas. Verso of title page.

5. Who is the publisher?
   TotalRecall Publications, Inc. Verso of title page

6. When was this edition published?
   2015. Verso of title page

7. Is the book part of a series?
   Learn library skills series. Front cover and title page

8. What is the ISBN?
   978 1 59095 433 1. Verso of title page

9. Is there a dedication?
   No dedication

10. Does the book include an index?
    Index mentioned on Contents page. Located at the end of the book.

11. Does the book have a glossary?
    Has a glossary. Located at the end of the book.

12. Does the book have a bibliography?
    Has a bibliography. Located at the end of the book.

EXERCISE 7.6

Access point: *Any part of a catalog or database record, or entry in a bibliography, that enables a user to find the resource*

Authority file: *A collection of authority records containing the preferred forms of headings for names, series and subjects*

Authorized access point: *In RDA, the preferred title or name to be used as an access point in a descriptive cataloging record*

Book number: *The numbers, letters or combination of numbers and letters used to distinguish an individual item from other items with the same classification number*

Call number: *A number on a library item consisting of a classification number, a book number and often a location symbol*

Classification number: *The number allocated to a resource to indicate its subject and group it with similar items*

Subject heading: *A heading which describes a subject and provides subject access to a catalog*

Variant access point: *In RDA cataloging, a non-preferred variation of a title or name. Known as a 'see reference' in AACR2, it provides a direction from an access point that is not used to an authorized access point that is used*

EXERCISE 7.7

1. Are the following terms acceptable as subject headings?
   a. 'Stand-up comedy'
      Yes
   b. 'Earthmovers'
      No, use 'Earthmoving machinery'
   c. 'Crops – Ecology'
      Yes
   d. 'Meat-eating animals'
      No, use 'Carnivorous animals'

2. What types of publications would you include under the subject heading 'Collectibles'?
   General works on any objects of interest to collectors, including mass-produced items of little intrinsic value (see scope note under Collectibles)

3. 'Community and school' is an accepted term in LCSH but 'Community and libraries' is not. What term would you use instead?
   'Libraries and community'

4. Is there a scope note under the term Psychological warfare?
   Yes. Here are entered general works dealing with methods used to undermine the morale of the civilian population and the military forces of an enemy country.

5. Would I find any information in a library catalog under the subject heading 'Chinaware'?
   No, use either 'Porcelain' or 'Pottery'

6. I found some information on Wedding etiquette in the catalog. Can you suggest some broader subject headings that would lead me to more information?
   'Etiquette', 'Marriage customs and rites'

Exercise 7.8

1a.	000	*Computer science, information, general works*
	060	*General organizations and museology*
	069	*Museology (Museum science)*
	069.1	*Museum services to patrons*
	069.13	*Circulation services*
	069.132	*Museum objects*
1b.	300	*Social sciences*
	340	*Law*
	341	*Law of nations*
	341.4	*Jurisdiction over physical space; human rights*
	341.48	*Human rights*
1c.	500	*Science*
	540	*Chemistry and allied sciences*
	541	*Physical chemistry*
	541.2	*Theoretical chemistry*
	541.24	*Atomic structure*
1d.	600	*Technology (Applied sciences)*
	610	*Medicine and health*
	612	*Human physiology*
	612.1	*Blood and circulation*
	612.13	*Blood vessels*
	612.133	*Arteries*
1e.	700	*The arts Fine and decorative arts*
	740	*Graphic arts and decorative arts*
	741	*Drawing and drawings*
	741.5	*Comic books, graphic novels, fotonovelas, cartoons, caricatures, comic strips*
	741.58	*Cartoon animation*
2.	Elephants	*599.67*
	Jackals	*599.772*
	Farming	*630*
	Library science	*020*

Exercise 7.9

1.
   a. World banking - *HG*
   b. The future of speed rail - *HE*
   c. Encyclopedia of sociology - *HM*
   d. Readings on international trade - *HF*

182   LEARN ABOUT INFORMATION

  e. The caste system in India - *HT*
  f. Government income and expenditure – *HJ*
2. a. QH540
   Periodicals, societies, congresses, serial publications
  b. QH540.4
   Dictionaries and encyclopedias
  c. QH540.8
   General works (Note that this is indented under History)
  d. QH541
   General works, treatises, and textbooks
  e. QH541.15.A-Z
   Special aspects of the subject as a whole, A-Z
  f. QH541.15.E25
   Economic ecology

EXERCISE 8.1

1a. What type of material is described in this catalog entry?
Monograph

1b. Who is the author?
Charles S. Carver and Michael F. Scheier

1c. Who published this item?
Pearson

1d. What is the date of publication?
2012

1e. Which edition is this publication?
Seventh edition

1f. Does the publication include an index?
Yes

1g. Does the publication contain references?
Yes

1h. What is this publication about?
Personality

1i. How could you find other books on this subject?
Look up the subject 'Personality', or the call number 'BF698.C22'

1j. Which classification scheme does this library use?
Library of Congress Classification

1k. Where would you find this publication on the shelf?
Shelf order in Central Library

1l. How many copies would you expect to find on the shelf?
One copy

ANSWERS   183

2a. What type of material is described in this catalog entry?
DVD

2b. Who produced this resource?
Chris Oxley and Malcolm Neaum; produced for NOVA by Joseph McMaster

2c. Who is the publisher of this item?
WGBH Boston Video

2d. What is this item about?
Sir Isaac Newton

2e. Does this item belong to a series?
No

2f. What is the playing time of this item?
56 minutes

3a. What type of material is described in this catalog entry?
Serial

3b. When was the first issue of this publication published?
1972

3c. If you needed vol. 39, no. 3 of this publication, would this library have a copy?
Yes

3d. What is the most recent issue received?
November 2014, volume 43, no. 6

3e. How would you find other items on this topic?
Look up the subject 'Sociology', or the call number 'HM1.C65'

3f. Has this publication changed its title?
Yes, it was formerly issued as the Book review section of the American sociology review.

EXERCISE 8.2

1. What is the title of the book written by Simon W. Bowmaker about the practice of economics research in 2012?
   'The art and practice of economics research : lessons from leading minds' – Look under author. Sort by date.

2. I have heard of a book titled 'Fundamentals of software testing' which was published in Hoboken, New Jersey in 2012 and I need to know who the author is?
   Bernard Homès - Look under title.

3. What is the name of the publisher of 'Total stock car racing'?
   Total/Sports Illustrated or Sports Illustrated. Look under title.

4. Does the book 'Principles of yacht design' which was published by International Marine/McGraw-Hill Education contain any illustrations? Who are the authors?
   Yes it contains illustrations (chiefly color). Authors are Lars Larsson, Rolf E Eliasson &

Michal Orych. Look under title.

5. Who publishes the electronic journal 'Geology'?
   Geological Society of America. Look under title.

6. Is there a list of music on the sound recording 'Treasure chest' by Decca produced in about 1957?
   Yes. Look under title. Full record

7. Has the 'Histochemical journal' changed its title?
   In 2003 the journal changed its title to Journal of molecular histology. Look under title.

8. What is the edition number of 'Clinical neuroanatomy' written by Stephen Waxman and published in 2013?
   Twenty-seventh edition. Look under title and author. Sort by date.

9. What is the ISBN for the book about Van Gogh written by Steven Naifeh and Gregory White Smith that was published in 2011 by Random House?
   ISBN is 9780375507489. Look under title and author. Sort by date.

10. When did the periodical 'Criminal behaviour and mental health' begin publication?
    Vol. 1, no. 1 1991. Look under title.

Exercise 8.3

Dictionary	*An alphabetically arranged publication containing information about words, meanings, derivations, spelling, pronunciation, syllabication and usage.*
Encyclopedia	*A systematic summary of all significant knowledge; a summary of the knowledge of one subject. Usually arranged alphabetically.*
Index	*A systematically arranged list which indicates the contents of a document or group of documents.*
Yearbook	*An annual publication containing current information in brief, descriptive and/or statistical form.*
Handbook	*A book written primarily for practitioners and serving as a book for constant revision or reference.*
Almanac	*An annual calendar with astronomical information and other data: a miscellany of useful facts and statistical information.*
Bibliography	*A list of related materials or resources, usually subject-related.*
Directory	*A list of names of residents, organizations or firms in a city, region, country or internationally, providing various details e.g., addresses; a list of members in a particular profession or trade.*
Atlas	*A volume of maps or charts with or without explanations.*
Gazetteer	*A geographical directory listing places, their locations and information about them.*
Biographical dictionary	*A listing of people, usually in alphabetical order of surname, providing details of dates, titles, birthplace, family, etc.*
Manual	*A book of instruction on doing, making or performing something.*

EXERCISE 8.4

Your specific answers will vary according to the source you've used but these are the type of sources you should have used.

1. What is the meaning of the word gecko?
   Use an English dictionary

2. Can you find a synonym for the word habitual?
   Use a thesaurus

3. Where can I find some illustrations of flags of the world?
   Use a general encyclopedia

4. Could you find some information on the life of Florence Nightingale?
   Use a general encyclopedia or a biographical dictionary

5. When was Pierre Elliott Trudeau the Prime Minister of Canada?
   Use a Canadian encyclopedia, a general encyclopedia or a biographical dictionary

6. What does the acronym GOTA stand for?
   Use a dictionary of acronyms

7. What is a palindrome?
   Use an English dictionary

8. Who was John Braine?
   Use a general encyclopedia or a biographical dictionary

9. Where would you find information about the experiences of African Americans in the United States?
   Use a specialized encyclopedia

10. What does smidgen mean?
    Use an English dictionary

11. What are John Kerry's hobbies?
    Use a biographical dictionary

12. What is the address of the Australian Tourist Commission in Los Angeles?
    Use a government directory or a Los Angeles telephone directory

13. When was the University of Oxford founded?
    Use an organizational directory or an encyclopedia

14. Where would I find some information about religion in Denmark?
    Use a general encyclopedia or a yearbook

15. What was the median household income in Luxembourg in 2011?
    Use a yearbook

16. When did the singer Placido Domingo make his operatic debut?
    Use a general encyclopedia or a biographical dictionary

17. When was David Cameron first elected to the British Parliament?
    Use a parliamentary handbook or a biographical dictionary

18. When did Rudyard Kipling die?
    Use a general encyclopedia or biographical dictionary

19. When did the tennis player, Serena Williams last win the Wimbledon title?
    Use a biographical dictionary or a current sports reference work

20. What is the main objective of UNESCO?
    Use an organizational directory or an encyclopedia

EXERCISE 8.5

Find the following information for each title.
   a. Type of bibliographic tool (e.g., national, trade)
   b. Publisher
   c. Frequency
   d. Subject coverage
   e. Format coverage
   f. Access points (how you search the database)

1. Books in print (http://www.booksinprint.com/)
   a. *Trade*
   b. *Bowker – a ProQuest affiliate*
   c. *Updated on a weekly basis*
   d. *All subjects*
   e. *Contains over 20 million global titles (in print, out of print, and forthcoming), including books, ebooks, audio books, and multimedia titles. U.S. edition—contains United States publications; Global edition—offers an expanded global view including US, Canada, Europe, UK, and Australia*
   f. *keyword, phrase, or specific data element (like an ISBN, title, author, publisher)*

2. British national bibliography (http://bnb.bl.uk/)
   a. *National*
   b. *British Library*
   c. *Updated on a weekly basis*
   d. *All subjects*
   e. *Lists the books and new journal titles published or distributed in the United Kingdom and Ireland since 1950. It also lists forthcoming book titles and hand-held electronic publications e.g., CD-ROMs, deposited with the Legal Deposit Office since 2003.*
   f. *Find titles by author, title, keyword, subject, ISBN/ISSN*

3. Canadiana (http://amicus.collectionscanada.ca/aaweb/aalogine.htm)
   a. *National*
   b. *Library and Archives Canada*
   c. *Updated on a weekly basis*
   d. *All subjects*
   e. *Published materials held at Library and Archives Canada and those located in over 1300 libraries across Canada. Contains over 30 million records for books, magazines,*

newspapers, government documents, theses, sound recordings, maps, electronic texts as well as items in braille and large print

 f. *Find titles by author, title, keyword, subject, ISBN/ISSN*

4. Ulrichsweb global serials directory (http://www.ulrichsweb.com/ulrichsweb/faqs.asp).
 a. *Trade*
 b. *SerialsSolutions – a ProQuest Company*
 c. *Updated on a weekly basis*
 d. *All subjects*
 e. *More than 300,00 periodicals of all types of academic and scholarly journals, Open Access publications, peer-reviewed titles, popular magazines, newspapers, newsletters and more from around the world. It covers all subjects, and includes publications that are published regularly or irregularly and that are circulated free of charge or by paid subscription.*
 f. *Find serials by ISSN, keyword, subject, title (keyword) or title (exact). Advanced Search or by browsing.*

EXERCISE 8.6

Question	Library Source
In what year did President John F. Kennedy die?	*Biographical dictionary*
How old was Peter Jennings when he died?	*Internet*
Does my library hold any books about Emily Dickinson? If my library doesn't, which libraries do?	*Library catalog / union catalog*
Where can I find a bibliography of poems from the First World War?	*Subject bibliography*
Are any works by Henry David Thoreau still in print?	*Trade bibliography*

EXERCISE 9.1

Alaimo, Katherine, Elizabeth Packnett, Richard A. Miles, and Daniel J. Kruger. 'Fruit and vegetable intake among urban community gardeners'. *Journal of Nutrition Education and Behavior* 40 (2) (2008): 94-101. Accessed Nov 27, 2014. doi:10.1016/j.jneb.2006.12.003.

Alexander, Stephanie. *Stephanie Alexander Kitchen Garden Foundation.* Last modified Nov 7, 2014. http://www.kitchengardenfoundation.org.au/.

Biggle, Jacob. *Biggle orchard book*. 1st ed. Philadelphia, Skyhorse Publishing, 2014. e-book.

Cox, Kenneth, and Ray Cox. *Scotland for gardeners: the ultimate guide to Scottish gardens, nurseries and garden centres.* New edition. Edinburgh, Burlinn, 2014.

Flottum, Kim. *The backyard beekeeper: an absolute beginner's guide to keeping bees in your yard and garden.* 3rd edition. Backyard series. Beverley, MA, Quarry Books, 2014.

The garden of words. Directed by Makoto Shinkai. Richmond, Victoria, Sentai filmworks, 2014. DVD, 116 min.

Grainger, Percy. *Country gardens.* [Wokingham, UK], Julian Dyer, 201-?. Piano roll.

Jaenke, Rachael L., Clare E. Collins, Philip J. Morgan, David R. Lubans, Kristen L. Saunders, and Janet M. Warren. 'The impact of a school garden and cooking program on boys' and girls' fruit and vegetable preferences, taste rating, and intake'. *Health Education & Behavior* 39 (2) (2012): 131-141. Accessed Nov 27, 2014. doi:10.1177/1090198111408301.

Langellotto, Gail Ann. 'What are the economic costs and benefits of home vegetable gardens?'. *Journal of Extension* 52 (2) (2014): 2-5. Accessed Nov 27, 2014. http://www.joe.org/joe/2014april/rb5.php.

Ondra, Nancy J. *Five-plant gardens: 52 ways to grow a perennial garden with just five plants.* North Adams, MA, Storey Publishing, 2013.

Phipps Conservatory and Botanical Gardens. *Your guide to Phipps Conservatory and Botanical Gardens.* Pittsburgh, Phipps Conservatory and Botanical Gardens, 2014. Map.

Rinne, Katherine. 'Garden hydraulics in pre-Sistine Rome: theory and practice'. Chapter 6 in *Technology and the garden,* edited by Michael G. Lee and Kenneth I. Helphand. 1st ed. Dumbarton Oaks colloquium on the history of landscape architecture 35. Washington, DC, Dumbarton Oaks, 2014.

EXERCISE 11.4

Library services which are unique to public libraries:
- *Community information*
- *Local history*
- *Literacy support*
- *Children's services – e.g., storytelling, holiday activities*
- *Extension services to remote users, housebound, aged, hospital patients*
- *Access to large print and talking books*
- *Clubs for various user groups*
- *Bookmobiles*

EXERCISE 11.5

The ways in which a public library may promote its services include:
- *Visits by schools, clubs*
- *Special events (e.g., authors' visits)*
- *Newspaper articles, especially in local newspapers*
- *Reviews of recently acquired material, placed in the local newspaper*
- *Open day tours*
- *Entry in local government annual report*
- *Publicity for fine amnesty periods*
- *Library as a venue for club activities.*

EXERCISE 13.2

	Library	Archive	Records Management Unit	Community Information Agency
What type of information is collected?	Print and non-print material, usually published commercially in wide range of subject areas, formats and levels	Material, usually not published, deemed to be of long-lasting value	Material considered of current value to parent organization	Material, usually in print, that provides up-to-date information on a limited range of topics
How is the information arranged?	Classified by subject, or in alphabetical order by author	Arranged in the order used by the depositing agency	Arranged by subject, controlled by a strict subject thesaurus	Often arranged in alphabetical order by subject
How do users find what information they require?	Searching the catalog or browsing open access shelves	By consulting catalogs, directories and finding aids	By accessing the subject thesaurus and file directories	Users ask for assistance
Can users retrieve the information themselves?	In most cases yes, or material is retrieved from closed access stacks by staff	No	In most cases, no	Not normally but sometimes agencies may provide brochures that can be taken away
Who are the users?	Members of the public (public libraries) or those who belong to the parent organization (special libraries), or academic institution (educational libraries)	Parent organization, researchers, or members of the public	Parent organization	Members of the public

Can the users borrow the material?	*In most libraries, users can borrow the majority of the material*	*No*	*Users can access the material for work-related enquiries*	*No*
Who looks after the material?	*Librarian, library technician*	*Archivist*	*Records manager, records clerk*	*Often volunteers, with professional supervision*

GLOSSARY

This glossary contains only those terms used in *Learn about information*. For a more comprehensive glossary, see Farkas, Lynn, *LibrarySpeak: a glossary of terms in librarianship and information management*.

abstract Also summary. A summary of the essential points of an article or literary work

academic library A library serving the information needs of the students and staff of a university or similar institution

access point A heading given to a catalog or database record or entry in a bibliography that enables a user to find the item

acquisition The process of adding to a library's collection by purchase, gift or exchange

archives 1. Records or historical documents that are preserved permanently because of their enduring value. 2. The storage area where archival material is kept. 3. An organization responsible for the care and control of archival material

bibliographic Related to books or other library materials

bibliographic element A distinct piece of bibliographic information which forms part of a catalog record

bibliographic tools Resources used to provide information about and access to books and other material (e.g., national bibliographies, trade bibliographies)

bibliography A list of related library materials or resources, usually subject-related

biographical dictionary or **biographical directory** A listing of people, usually in alphabetical order of surname, providing details of dates, titles, birthplace, family etc.

blog A regularly updated website or web page, often run by an individual or small group, that is written in an informal or conversational style

call number A number on a library item consisting of a classification number, a book number and often a location symbol

catalog A list of library materials contained in a collection, a library or a group of libraries, arranged according to some definite plan

cataloger A person who prepares catalog entries and maintains a catalog so that library materials can be retrieved efficiently

cataloging The preparation of bibliographic information for catalog records. Cataloging consists of descriptive cataloging, subject cataloging and classification

cataloging tools Publications of the international cataloging rules and standards, including *Resource description and access (RDA)*, *Library of Congress subject headings (LCSH)*, *Library of Congress classification (LCC)*, *Dewey decimal classification (DDC)*

citation tools Capture bibliographic information about resources, create bibliographies, and add footnotes. Some citation tools allow you to share references with others.

classification Libraries: A system for arranging library materials according to subject. Records management: The process by which files and documents are categorized or grouped to facilitate retrieval

classification number Number allocated to a library item to indicate a subject

classification scheme A particular scheme for arranging library materials according to subject (e.g., Dewey Decimal Classification, Library of Congress Classification)

closed reserve Also reserve collection, restricted loan, short loan. A collection of material in high demand, usually in a teaching institution, whose access is controlled and whose loan periods are shorter than normal library loans

collection development Planning the acquisition of material to build a library collection for the short to long term, to meet the needs of library users

collective title The title of an item containing several works

commercial information agency An information supplier operated for profit

community information agency An agency which provides community information not for profit

competency The specification of the knowledge and skill and the application of that knowledge and skill to the standard of performance required in employment

competency standards A grouping of units of competency that expresses the requirements to be competent at a variety of levels

contents page The page at the front of a book or serial which lists the contents in the order in which they appear

copy cataloging The process of copying cataloging details from an existing catalog record, and adding local location and holdings details

copyright The exclusive right given by law to authors, composers or publishers to sell, reproduce or publish a work during a stated period of time

current awareness bulletin CAB. A publication provided by a library to keep users up-to-date with information in their interest areas

current awareness service CAS. A service provided by a library to keep users up-to-date with information in their interest areas

database A collection of records, usually in machine-readable format, each record being the required information about one resource

descriptive cataloging The process which describes an item, identifies and formats access points

Dewey Decimal Classification DDC. A classification scheme, devised by Melvil Dewey in 1873, using numbers to represent subjects

dictionary An alphabetically arranged publication containing information about words, meanings, derivations, spelling, pronunciation, syllabication and usage

digital repository A mechanism for managing and storing digital content. Some repositories take in particular items (such as theses or journal articles), while others accept any scholarly work produced by staff and students at the institution

directory A list of names of residents, organizations or firms in a city, region, country or internationally, providing various details (e.g., addresses; a list of members of a particular profession or trade)

discovery layer A library user interface using specialized software to simultaneously search the library's catalog, journal subscription services, institutional repositories, online resources etc. This provides a single point of access to the library's full collection, across bought, licensed and digital materials

document delivery The delivery of published and unpublished information by conventional and electronic means, including electronic mail and facsimile transmission, often part of the interlibrary loan process

encyclopedia A systematic summary of all significant knowledge; a summary of the knowledge of one subject. Usually arranged alphabetically

endprocessing The preparation of an item for use in the library or for loan, after it has been cataloged

ephemera Material of current interest which is expected to be stored for a limited time (e.g., pamphlets, cuttings)

ethics A system of moral principles by which actions or proposals may be judged right or wrong

federated search A technology that lets users search multiple databases simultaneously using one search query, then view the results in a single integrated list

folksonomy A user-generated system of classifying and organizing online content into different categories by the use of metadata such as electronic tags

Freedom of Information FOI. The legal right to see documents that are held by government departments and agencies

frequency Interval between issues of a serial (e.g., weekly, quarterly)

gazetteer A geographical directory listing places, their locations and information about them

government publication A document prepared for or by a government agency which is published and distributed for public information

grey literature Informally published materials, such as reports or working papers, that may be difficult to trace through conventional acquisitions sources because they are not published commercially or not widely accessible

handbook A concise ready reference source of information for a particular field of knowledge

hierarchy 1. The ranked order of subjects in a classification scheme. 2. The order of subordinate bodies in a multilevel corporate body

imprint Publication details—place, publisher, date of publication

index 1. An alphabetical list of terms or topics in a work, usually found at the back. 2. A systematically arranged list which indicates the contents of a document or group of documents

indexing service A periodical publication which regularly and systematically indexes the contents of periodical and sometimes other publications

information Knowledge in any field, gained by experience or instruction

information agency An organization which provides access to information (e.g., a library, an archive)

information broker A person who conducts a search for information on behalf of another person

information literacy The ability to recognize a need for information, and then to find, organize and use information

information package A format in which information is presented (e.g., monograph, poster, computer file)

information policy A plan for provision of and access to information in an organization or region

information retrieval Finding information in a library or collection

information technology IT. The acquisition, processing, storage and dissemination of information by means of computers and telecommunications

in-house system An information system established within an institution to meet the needs of its own staff

interlibrary loan ILL. A loan made by one library to another for the use of an individual, including the provision of a photocopy of the original work requested

joint author A writer who collaborates with one or more others in the preparation of a work

joint-use library A library which serves more than one user community (e.g., a joint school and public library)

journal A periodical issued by an institution, corporation or learned society containing current information and reports of activities or works in a particular field

knowledge Understanding gained through study or experience

learning resource center An area housing a collection of learning resources, usually in a school or college. Used as an alternative name for a school or college library

legal deposit The legal right of certain libraries to receive a free copy of each item published in a country or state

librarian A person with a library qualification recognized as professional by the relevant library association, or performing work at a professional level

librarianship The profession of the people who staff libraries and are involved in the management of libraries and library services

library 1. A collection of books and other materials for reading, study or reference. 2. A place housing a collection of materials for reading, study or reference, or from which to borrow

Library of Congress Classification A classification scheme developed by the Library of Congress, using numbers and letters

Library of Congress Subject Headings The authoritative list of subject headings compiled and maintained by the Library of Congress

library technician A person with a qualification in librarianship recognized as paraprofessional by the relevant library association, or performing work at a paraprofessional level

listserv A type of discussion group on the Internet. Listservs tend to be more professional or academic than general

MARC Machine readable cataloging. A system developed by the Library of Congress in 1966

so that libraries can share machine-readable bibliographic data

metadata Descriptive information used to describe and provide access to information resources, especially Internet sites and documents

mobile library or bookmobile A collection of library materials able to be transported to various locations to provide a library service

monograph A publication either complete in one part or in a finite number of separate parts

monograph in series A monograph which is part of a series with a common series title

national bibliography A listing of the publications of a country, about that country, by the residents of that country, in the language of that country

national library A library maintained out of government funds and serving the nation as whole. It is usually the country's legal deposit library, and collects and preserves the nation's literature

national union catalog A listing of the holdings of a large number of libraries in a country

network Two or more libraries or other organizations which exchange information

newspaper A printed publication issued regularly, usually daily or weekly, containing news, comment, features and advertising

newspaper cutting An article cut from a newspaper. Usually filed in a vertical file or photocopied and sent to identified library users

non-book material Also non-print material. Material other than printed materials (e.g., audiovisual material, computer software)

online portal An entry point to the Internet that provides access to electronic information including websites, ftp sites, databases and indexes to print resources in a subject area such as agriculture

OPAC Online public access catalog. A computer-based catalog which library users access via terminals

open access library Holds electronic resources that are free of charge with unrestricted access via the Internet, usually under a Creative Commons Licence

original cataloging Cataloging done for the first time, using cataloging tools to create the record

paraprofessional A person trained to assist librarians and able to perform tasks requiring significant knowledge in librarianship, but without a professional (i.e., degree) qualification. Can include library assistants, library officers, library technicians

periodical A serial with a distinctive title intended to appear in successive parts at stated and regular intervals. Often used as a synonym for serial

podcast A digital recording of music, news or other media that can be downloaded from the internet to a portable media player

primary source A document that provides first-hand knowledge of an event, including personal papers, photographs, etc.

professional Having a university or equivalent qualification in librarianship or information management, and performing work at a professional level

profile An outline of the interest area/s of a user or a group of users. Used by the library to identify new information of interest to particular users

provenance The archival principle of not intermingling records of different creators

public library A library funded by government which provides library services to all sections of the community

public services Also client services, reader services, reference services. Direct services to library users, including circulation, interlibrary loan, bibliographic instruction, and reference services

reader education Also bibliographic instruction, library orientation, reader instruction, user education. Helping people to derive the most benefit from using the library

readers' advisor A library staff member who advises readers on their choice of books and generally assists in the use of the resources of the library

reader services Also client services, public services, reference services. Direct services to library users, including circulation, interlibrary loan, bibliographic instruction, and reference services

ready reference query A question requiring factual information from one simple source

records management The control of the administrative records of an organization

reference collection A collection of books intended to be referred to rather than read. Usually not for loan outside the library

reference services Also reader services. Services to library users including reader education, meeting users' requests for specific information and assistance and the management of the use and loan of library material and equipment

reference work 1. Also reference book. A work intended to be referred to rather than read. 2. The work of the library which provides assistance to users seeking information

regional library A public library serving a district usually across local government boundaries

repository A place where material, for example archival material, is stored

reserve collection Also closed reserve, restricted loan, short loan. A collection of material in high demand, usually in a teaching institution, whose access is controlled and whose loan periods are shorter than normal library loans

resource sharing The sharing of material between libraries—for example where an expensive item is purchased by one library on the understanding that users of one or more other libraries have access to it

RSS, RSS feed A 'push' technology in which online publishers send changes of frequently updated website content directly to users, eliminating the need for the user to check the website regularly

school librarian Also teacher librarian. A librarian who manages a school library and offers a library service to students and staff of a school

school library A library in a school which offers a library service to students and staff

search engine Software that locates information in a database or set of databases, especially on the Internet

search strategy 1. The approach adopted to finding information on a particular topic. 2. The search statements used to answer an enquiry

secondary source A work that reports or interprets an event using first-hand documents

serial A publication issued in successive parts and intended to be continued indefinitely

series A number of works related to each other by the fact that they have a collective title, as well as each work having its own title proper

shared cataloging Also cooperative cataloging. Sharing of catalog records by participating libraries

short loan Also closed reserve, reserve collection, restricted loan. A collection of material in high demand, usually in a teaching institution, whose access is controlled and whose loan periods are shorter than normal library loans

social media A dedicated website or other application that allows people to create, share or exchange information, ideas, pictures or videos in a virtual community or network

special library A library specializing in a limited subject area. Usually maintained by a corporation, association or government agency

standard 1. A statement of what is expected of an individual performing a particular occupational role. It includes an 'element' of competence which describes what the individual should be able to do, and performance criteria which describe the standards of performance required for the successful achievement of the element of competence. 2. A criterion by which services and programs may be measured or assessed

state library The government-funded library of a state or territory which aims to provide library services to the whole state, including support of public libraries

subject cataloging Describing the content of a work using subject headings and a classification number

subject heading A heading which describes a subject and provides subject access to a catalog

teacher librarian Also school librarian. A librarian who manages a school library and offers a library service to students and staff

technical services Library services which deal with the bibliographic control—including acquisition, cataloging and endprocessing—of library material

tertiary source A guide to the literature of a particular field (e.g., a bibliography of bibliographies, a directory of directories, etc.)

title page The page which provides the most complete information about the author and title, and is used as the most authoritative source of cataloging data

trade bibliography A listing of books available for sale in a country, together with details of publishers etc., needed for purchase

union catalog Catalog of the holdings of more than one library

Universal Decimal Classification UDC. A classification scheme developed by the International Federation for Information and Documentation (FID) by expanding Dewey Decimal Classification. It offers the most specific classification for specialized collections and is widely used in special libraries

verification Checking data to confirm bibliographic details

vertical file A collection of current material including pamphlets and newspaper clippings. Usually arranged in subject order in a filing cabinet

virtual library A library whose primary resources are electronic, and which provides access for its users to databases, images etc., including via other information providers

website A set of related web pages served from a single web domain

wiki 1. Server software that allows users freely to create and edit web page content using any web browser. 2. A website or database developed collaboratively by a community of users, allowing any user to add or edit content. 3. (v) to research a topic on a wiki, or to contribute to a wiki

yearbook An annual publication containing current information in brief, descriptive and/or statistical form

BIBLIOGRAPHY

Beheshti, Jamshid & Large, Andrew (2013). *The information behavior of a new generation: children and teens in the 21st century.* Lanham, Md. : Scarecrow Press, Inc.

Bowden, John (2011). *Writing a report: how to prepare, write & present really effective reports.* 9th edition. Oxford : How To.

Bradley, Phil (2015). *Social media for creative libraries.* London : Facet Publishing.

Cassell, Kay Ann & Hiremath, Uma (2013). *Reference and information services: an introduction.* Third edition. Chicago : Neal-Schuman Publishers Inc.

Crawford, Walt (2014). *Successful social networking in public libraries.* Chicago : American Library Association.

Eisenberg, M., Lowe, C., & Spitzer, K. (2004). *Information literacy: essential skills for the information age.* 2nd. edition. Westport, Conn. : Libraries Unlimited.

Farkas, Lynn (2015). *LibrarySpeak: a glossary of terms in librarianship and information management.* International edition. Friendswood, Texas : TotalRecall Publications.

Floridi, Luciano (2010). *Information: a very short introduction.* Oxford : Oxford University Press.

Ford, Nigel (2015). *Introduction to information behaviour.* London : Facet Publishing.

Hamill, Lois (2013). *Archives for the lay person: a guide to managing cultural collections.* Lanham, Md. : AltaMira.

Hill, Jennie (2010). *The future of archivist and recordkeeping: a reader.* London : Facet Publishing.

Kietzmann, Jan H., Kristopher Hermkens, Ian P. McCarthy, Bruno S. Silvestre (2011). "Social media? Get serious! Understanding the functional building blocks of social media". *Business Horizons* 54: 241–251. doi:10.1016/j.bushor.2011.01.005.

Landis, Cliff (2010). *A social networking primer for librarians.* London : Facet Publishing.

Lanning, Scott (2012). *Concise guide to information literacy.* Santa Barbara, California : Libraries Unlimited.

Polanka, Sue (2012). *No shelf required 2: use and management of electronic books.* Chicago : American Library Association.

Rubin, Rhea Joyce, (2011). *Defusing the angry patron: a how-to-do-it manual for librarians.* New York : Neal-Schuman Publishers Inc.

Secker, Jane, Boden, Debbi & Price, Gwyneth (2007). *The information literacy cookbook: ingredients, recipes and tips for success.* Oxford : Chandos Publishing.

Walton, Geoff; Pope, Alison (2011). *Information literacy: infiltrating the agenda, challenging minds.* Oxford : Chandos Publishing.

Weir, Ryan O. (2012). *Managing electronic resources: a LITA guide.* Chicago : ALA TechSource, an imprint of the American Library Association.

INDEX

academic libraries, 125-128
archives, 145-147
bibliographic
    elements, 63-76
    tools, 79-92
bibliographies, 90
bibliography, preparing 96-98
catalog, 69, 78-79
cataloging, 69-73
citation tools, 102
classification, 72-73
client satisfaction, 151-153
communication, 3, 154-155
community information agencies, 149
competency standards, 159
complaints, 156-157
copyright, 165
current awareness services, 110, 133
databases, 42-44, 46, 47-51
descriptive cataloging, 69
Dewey Decimal Classification, 72
dictionaries, 86
digital repositories, 126-127
directories, 40, 86
discovery layers, 40-42
electronic resources, 29, 37-51, 53-62, 97
encyclopedias, 86
ethics, 162-163
federated searches, 40-42
Freedom of Information, 167
geographical sources, 86
handbooks, 86
indexes, 40
information agencies, 141-150
information
    creation of, 6
    dissemination of, 6
    evaluation of, 22-24
    good, 4
    literacy, 15-28
    nature of, 1-8
    organization of, 27
    overload, 27-28
    packages, 29-36
    policies, 13
    poor, 4
    presentation of, 27, 93-106
    process, 18-27
    skills, 17
    sources of, 6, 19-20, 21
    users of, 9-12
    value of, 8
interlibrary loan, 109, 137, 138, 160
interlibrary loan code, 109
joint-use libraries, 121, 123-124
legislation, 165-168
libraries
    aims, 107
    staffing, 111-112
    standards, 159-161
    structure of, 108-111
    types of, 108, 115-134
Library of Congress Subject Headings, 70, 79
Library of Congress Classification, 72
loans, 109
MARC 137, 160
metadata, 1, 134
networks, 135-139
non-print resources, 30, 97-98
OCLC, 136
online portals, 38
open access libraries, 127
oral presentations, 102-105
paraprofessional staff, 112
print resources, 29-30, 97
privacy, 166, 167
professional
    staff, 112
    statements, 161
Public Lending Right, 167-168

public libraries, 119, 120-123, 131, 138, 149
public relations, 111, 122
public services, 108-111
reader education, 109-110
records management, 142-144
reference
    collection, 85-86
    services, 110
report writing, 94-96
school libraries, 129-131
search engines, 37-38
search functions, 47-51
search strategy, 19-20, 50
social media, 53-62
    benefits, 60-61
    functions of, 58-59
    safe use of, 60
    types of, 53-54
special libraries, 132-134
standards, 159-161
state libraries, 119, 121, 138
subject cataloging, 70
surveys, 151-152
technical services, 111
union catalogs, 79, 136, 137
Universal Decimal Classification, 73, 133
virtual educational institutions, 127-128
websites, 22-23, 42, 46, 47-51
yearbooks, 86

LEARN LIBRARY SKILLS SERIES

This series of paperback workbooks introduces skills needed by library science students and library technicians, as well as librarians seeking refresher materials or study guides for in-service training classes. Each book teaches essential professional skills in a step-by-step process, accompanied by numerous practical examples, exercises and quizzes to reinforce learning, and an appropriate glossary.

Learn About Information
International Edition ©2015
Helen Rowe
ISBN: 9781590954331 Paperback

Learn Basic Library Skills
International Edition ©2015
Helen Rowe and Trina Grover
ISBN: 9781590954348 Paperback

Learn Cataloging the RDA Way
International Edition ©2015
Lynn Farkas and Helen Rowe
ISBN: 9781590954355 Paperback

Learn Dewey Decimal Classification (Edition 23)
International Edition ©2015
Lynn Farkas
ISBN: **9781590954362** Paperback

Learn Management Skills for Libraries and Information Agencies
International Edition ©2015
Jacinta Ganendran
ISBN: 9781590954379 Paperback

Learn Library of Congress Classification
International Edition ©2015
ISBN: 9781590954386 Paperback

Learn Library of Congress Subject Access
International Edition ©2015
Lynn Farkas
ISBN 9781590954393 Paperback

Learn Reference Work
International Edition ©2015
ISBN: 9781590954416 Paperback

LIBRARY SCIENCE TITLES

LibrarySpeak:
A Glossary of Terms in Librarianship and Information Technology,
International Edition ©2015
Lynn Farkas
ISBN: 9781590954423 Paperback

My Mentoring Diary:
A Resource for the Library and Information Professions
Revised Edition ©2015
Ann Ritchie and Paul Genoni
ISBN: 9781590954430 Paperback

Quality in Library Service:
A Competency-Based Staff Training Program
International Edition ©2015
Jennifer Burrell and Brad McGrath
ISBN: 9781590954447 Paperback

TOTALRECALL PUBLICATIONS, INC.
1103 Middlecreek,
Friendswood, TX 77546-5448

Phone: (281) 992-3131
email: Sales@TotalRecallPress.com
Online: www.totalrecallpress.com

www.ingramcontent.com/pod-product-compliance
Lightning Source LLC
Chambersburg PA
CBHW081102070526
44584CB00021B/3174